GANNET
The Story of a Terrier

J. N. P. WATSON

ASHFORD, BUCHAN & ENRIGHT
Southampton

Published by Ashford, Buchan & Enright, 1 Church Road,
Shedfield, Hampshire SO3 2HW

British Library Cataloguing in Publication Data

Watson, J. N. P. (John N. P.)
Gannet.
I. Title
823'.914 [F]

ISBN 1–85253–208–4

Typeset by Words & Spaces, Portsmouth
**Printed and bound in Great Britain by
Hartnolls Ltd, Bodmin**

By the same author

The World's Greatest Horse Stories (an Anthology)
Captain-General and Rebel Chief: The Life of James, Duke of Monmouth
Sefton: The Story of a Cavalry Horse
The World's Greatest Dog Stories (an Anthology)
Lionel Edwards: Master of the Sporting Scene
The World of Polo: Past and Present
Collecting Sporting Art (editor)
Millais: Three Generations in Nature, Art and Sport
A Concise Guide to Polo
Blue and Scarlet: an Autobiography
Horse and Carriage: the Pageant of Hyde Park
etc.

This story is dedicated to my terrier, Grizel, and to the memory of her daughter, Gannet, the runt of the litter and very accident-prone, who died on the night of the 28th November 1984. And also to Claudia French, dog lover *par excellence*, on her seventeenth birthday.

When pups are born on a stormy night,
Life is going to be cruel and bitter,
Life is going to be one long fight,
For the smallest one, the runt of the litter
Old country saying

PROLOGUE

April 2

She had been known as old Grizel since she was two years old. This was to distinguish her from a daughter by her first mate. Old Grizel's piebald muzzle, fair testimony to her service in bolting many foxes for the Westdown hunt, was criss-crossed up to her eyes and ears with the scars of fox-bites incurred in the bowels of the earth when the men with spades had withdrawn and she had descended, time and again, with the passion of one whose only real object in life was to engage with a fox, yap in his face, hold him at bay or turn him and bolt him; and so before she reached the age of three, she had earned the reputation of being the best the hunt had ever had. Smart chestnut red-and-white with short straight legs and a sharp head, small for her breed but with very well-developed shoulders, loins and neck muscles and great depth through the heart, she was still as easy on the eye of showing judges as she was good in her work.

The night old Grizel gave birth to the second litter of her breeding career a spring storm raged, a storm of such proportions that — as Ted Jennings put it afterwards — the thunderclaps were like bleedin' 'owitzer batteries. The rain's knitting needles beat with unremitting fury against the windows; the gale whistled and raged into every corner of the hunt kennels at Owlhurst, through the yards and into the boiler room, the flesh hovel and the lodging-rooms, where the melodrama of the thunder and lightning kept some of the foxhounds waiting continuously until dawn, while every now and then came a wild neighing from the stables.

Close to the foxhounds' stone-built kennels complex stood the much less stoutly protected terrier pens. Two window panes near old Grizel's whelping-box, which leaned right into the prevailing wind, rattled until the early hours and finally shattered, letting torrents of rain on to her straw. She edged away into the only remaining dry corner, her four puppies thinly squeaking, as they scrambled, blinder than moles, after the succour of her nipples and the comfort of her steaming warmth. She looked up, growling from the back of her throat at the aperture where the rain came in, as though it were a living enemy, and pushed further into her dry corner, while the pink, blunt, velvet-soft snouts fed from her belly, and the spring of her elastic tongue worked as though the whelps' lives depended upon it — incessantly and frantically on their sticky bodies, so minute she could lift them on the end of it. Her whole being concentrated on those four tiny particles of life, two bitches and two dogs.

The litter comprised quite a mixture of colour and marking. One of the puppies, taking after its sire, was liver-and-white; another, a throw-back, bore a single black patch on his side and two black ears. The other two, one bitch, one dog, were chestnut-red-and-white like their dam. Of these two the bitch was significantly smaller than the others, a frail-looking puppy, the runt of the litter; and her coat was so short and thin that, at first sight, you might have thought her naked. But on closer inspection you might have noticed that she was likely to emerge, in addition to her main red-and-white, with an unusual red mottling, while on her blind, blunt face, a pretty, if faintly discernible, pattern of black reached from a point above her black muzzle and — divided by the white streak on the centre of her head — encircled her eyes. At the beginning of her life those delicate markings, which would gradually become more pronounced, were her only redeeming feature. Soon to be celebrated as 'Gannet', she is the subject of this account.

CHAPTER ONE

Old Grizel's tongue was still working without a pause on her puppies, when the time arrived for hound exercise and she heard a light gumboot tread in the yard. She knew those footsteps as well as any in the world. They belonged to Rose Maxwell, the kennel-girl. Behind Rose's step was a man's, pleasingly recognizable if not so familiar to Grizel. It was that of a young and newly qualified veterinary surgeon called Luke Peterson, who frequently joined in on hound exercise, not so much in order to keep his professional eye on the hounds or even because he was particularly fond of walking — but much more because he was fond of Rose Maxwell.

By now the rain had stopped and the wind stilled and the sky was touched with pink and gold to herald a clear April day. Only the puddles on the flagstone yard, the wreckage of the pens and the wet on Grizel's straw bore witness to the turbulent night. Her stumpy tail switched, her tongue flicked coyly round her scarred nose as the door of her whelping-box opened.

'Ooh, Luke, come and see — Griz with a family! And there was Ted Jennings and me swearing they wouldn't be here till Saturday.' Rose, on her haunches, glanced up at the vet 'They're all right, are they?'

Peterson, a reserved freckled young man with grave eyes and short brown hair, leaned past her and made a cursory inspection. 'They're fine . . . small litter. She's done her job well. Her second lot, is it?'

'That's right. Oh, clever, clever Griz.' Rose, who was then only eighteen, was a large lithe good-looking girl. Her heavy mop of gold hair was held back with a cotton scarf. 'But, oh Griz, what a terrible night to choose for it . . . I'll get you something to eat.'

She returned after a minute with bowls of milk and chopped meat. Grizel got up, turned aside from her young and ate and drank copiously, while Rose started picking out the bits of broken window-pane and pushing aside some of the wet straw. Then across her shoulder she heard the huntsman's footsteps, his habitual grunts and heavy breathing and Luke Peterson's greeting: 'Hullo Ted, just take a look at what Rose has found: your Grizel with four fat pups. Thought you said we shouldn't expect them till Saturday.'

Ted Jennings peered over Rose's shoulder. 'Well I'll be blowed, three days early. Must've had 'em in the storm . . . Ain't they a picture, eh?'

With his pointed nose, convex profile and bright, knowing eye, Jennings looked a bit like an old dog-fox that has tricked the hounds a thousand times. By then fifty-four of his sixty-nine years had been devoted to hunt service, not counting his call-up time. His stoop and his gnarled fingers spoke of a man beginning to feel the grip of arthritis. He was rather deaf, too. His appointment with the Westdown was as kennel-huntsman and first whipper-in, because the Master, Major Mayne 'carried the horn' now, while Jennings 'turned hounds to him', as the jargon has it, an arrangement which suited Jennings well in the autumn of his life. On hunting days an amateur, a young farmer called Martin Eliot, acted as second whipper-in.

'I can't wait to show Martin,' bubbled Rose. 'He's got a very soft spot for Grizel.'

Instinctively, Jennings who judged that Eliot had an even softer spot for Rose, gave Luke Peterson a quick anxious glance and noticed the grimace on the vet's face. Then he returned to the puppies. 'Y'see the little 'un? Lot smaller, ain't she? Good job there's only four. Otherwise little 'un might get bullied out of the way and starve.' He turned to Luke. 'Weak-looking enough as it is, don't you think?'

The young vet was non-committal: 'There's no doubt it's the runt of the litter.'

Jennings stroked a thumb down the grey stubble of his cheek, then began quoting, quietly and thoughtfully, groping to remember the words:

When pups is born on a stormy night
Life is goin' to be . . . cruel and bitter.
Life is goin' to be one long fight
For the . . . littlest 'un, the runt of the litter.

Rose, who was now holding an armful of fresh straw for Grizel, laughed, and so did Luke: 'Where'd you pick that one up, Ted?'

'Where'd I what?' He had been deafened in the Normandy campaign.

'Where did you pick it up — find it?' she shouted.

'Never heard of it? Bit of old south country folklore that is, and, mark my words, I've known it come true more'n once or twice . . . Let's get along then, time for exercise an' all. Grizel can wait.'

So saying the old huntsman stumped off to open the foxhounds' lodging-rooms, letting them cascade into the yard like huge bees pouring from the hive when the sun comes out, a canine torrent of black-tan-and-white, all twenty-one-and-a-half couple of them — every one the Westdown hunt owned that was not 'sick or sorry'. Rose — with Luke — stayed at the terrier pen for another moment or two, gazing mesmerized by the beauty of the red-and-white terrier and her new-born family. Then, very gently, she picked up the runt and, with laughing lips on its lick-damp forehead, she whispered: '*Life is going to be* — what did he say? — *cruel and bitter; life is going to be one long fight for the smallest one, the runt of the litter.*' Replacing it alongside its brothers and sister she added: 'We'll have to look after you, won't we?'

'Confess it, Rose,' said Luke, 'you're almost as superstitious as Ted!'

She flashed her smile at him in reply.

'Come along then, Rosie!' Jennings's voice resounded from the yard. 'Hounds is waitin'.'

Leaving Grizel and her puppies to work out their own salvation for the next couple of hours, Jennings, Luke and Rose cycled for a mile or so down the Old Shepherd's Way. Rose and Luke led, with Jennings behind, and, in between, the trotting pack, a body of piston-rod thighs and waving sterns, every now and then one of them dropping back to relieve nature, then galloping to catch up. When they reached the end of the lane, huntsman, kennel-girl and vet locked their bicycles by the stile with the public footpath sign that pointed up to the broad open downs.

At the top Luke stopped for a second, looking down at the sea, blue and still, took a deep breath and, as he walked on, turned to Rose: 'How bright and lovely everything is up here when the sun's out after a storm.'

Rose in jeans and open shirt, had transferred her scarf from her head to her neck and the faint breeze drew wisps of gold hair across her cheeks as she answered him.

'This is easily my favourite exercise area.' She glanced

across her shoulder at the pack. 'I'm sure the hounds like it best here, too.'

Indeed Rose appeared to be more interested in the hounds than she was in Luke Peterson. Certainly her thoughts were of them now. Out of the hunting season the hounds were never more exuberant than when they were on exercise, feeling the strength and agility of their limbs and receiving the odours of the wild, especially those delectable illicit scents of rabbit, deer, badger and squirrel and, occasionally, that most tantalising of nectars, fox.

The hounds' euphoria added to Rose's; she loved to share their high spirits and, as one of nature's staunchest devotees, there was no place in the world she cherished more than the downs in springtime with the gorse shining bright as sunbeams, the scabious in tiny bud, and its particular sounds — the songbirds twittering, the cawing in the rookeries, the larks chorusing high above their grass-cupped nests, the urgent cries of the parent blackbirds, the chattering of the starling flocks and, once in a while, the croak of old Jennings coming from behind, rating young hounds that had the impudence to scamper after a rabbit: 'Ware leave it, Bountiful! Bike, come bike will yer, Gimlet! 'Ware rabbit!' It was so glorious up there just now with wafts of sea-salt air, the sparkling Channel to the south and the sylvan weald to the north, the bramble thickets all incipient lime-green, the primroses and celandine smiling up from the sheep-cropped turf which dazzled from the night's rain, and her beloved hounds pattering at her heels. And already brimstones and orange tips and chalk blues fluttered over the pasture; it was going to be a wonderful summer for butterflies!

'You'd be happy working at Owlhurst for ever, I suppose?' Luke asked.

'Oh, I don't know.'

Having loved animals, dogs above all, for as long as she could remember, employment with them was essential to Rose's life. Luke's question prompted her to think about her future. In the previous autumn she had completed her year and won her certificate at that fine institution, the Bell Mead Kennelmaid Training School, an offshoot of the Battersea Dogs' Home lying close to Runnymede. Besides general care and management, she had been taught anatomy, nutrition, whelping, nursing and first aid — in short, everything embodied in loving dogs and having a pride in them. She had taken the job with the Westdown hunt because it was less than two miles from her home with her widowed father, whom she looked after.

Rose did not have a lot of time to herself in those days. Not that she minded; far from it. She adored dogs, the more the merrier. There were forty-eight foxhounds, or rather twenty-four couple, in kennels at Owlhurst, not to mention three hunt terriers.

She had only known Luke about a month. She liked his company well enough, but he was a bit too anxious for her liking to keep up this chat with her, and that April day happened to be one of those days when, as she put it, she 'just wanted to absorb the spring beauty.' So his attempts at conversation were not very productive.

'Sorry the hunting season's over, are you, Rose?'

They were circling a two-acre stand of beeches on the open summit of the downs now, a covert that was generally described by the *cognoscenti* as 'a sure find' during the season.

'Not at all', Rose replied. 'Change of routine's good for me.' Turning from him she looked back at the hounds again and gave Jennings a quick wave. She thought about her first hunting season, just over, and of the five months of long daily hound exercise which lay ahead until cubbing resumed in September. She rarely went out hunting herself. There just wasn't time, what with preparing the hounds' evening meal and seeing that everything else was ready in the kennels for their homecoming. She didn't at all mind missing the day's sport.

Luke tried to cajole her into talk again. 'You haven't had any qualms about hunting, I hope? I mean the ethics of the sport?'

'Not really.'

'What does "not really" mean?'

'It means I'm quite happy about it.' Rose took the view that, if foxes must be culled — and culled they must — there was no kinder method than hunting with hounds. Shooting, trapping and gassing were, in her opinion, the cruel methods of fox control, whereas hunting ensured a clean death or a clean escape. Rose rationalised, as she found herself rationalising again that April morning, that hunting was the only means of control that kept the fox population at a reasonable level, the only method that did not decimate that beautiful species.

Considering there was a strong lobby against hunting and

she herself, a foxhounds' kennel-girl, was such a self-professed ardent animal-lover, she had practised her arguments in its defence time and again: hunting was the natural way to control foxes, she told her non-hunting friends. The fox was once the prey of the wolf pack, and, although man destroyed the wolf, it behoved him to find the natural alternative. On the other hand a countryside without foxes would be an impoverished countryside. Foxhunting sorted out the old and sick foxes while more often than not the young, sharp ones got away. Rose knew that, in non-hunting countries, there were scarcely any foxes to be seen, nearly all of them having succumbed to the guns and traps and poisons of the gamekeeper and poultry farmers and the snares of that even more iniquitous exploiter, the pelt-trapper. the hunts did their best to monitor the foxes in their countries and to prevent shooting and trapping.

So it was a sport? Rose paused in her reflections and shrugged. If an exciting and healthy diversion was a by-product of the cull, all well and good. It was a fine British heritage. Above all, so far as she was concerned, it was the *raison d'être* of foxhounds; it was their ecstasy. What better reason could there be for hunting that that, she asked herself.

They were on the south side of the crest now, looking down the slope, forty-five degrees to the sea on which just one vessel, a ferry boat with gulls in its wake, stood like an exclamation mark on the great sparkling turquoise and white expanse. Luke, eager for her attention, continued to shoot enquiring glances in her direction, and followed up his last question with another: 'Seeing you with Grizel and her new-born litter this morning, made me wonder how you feel about digging foxes and well . . . terrier work in general?'

'Oh, I hate it!' she shuddered, and this was the subject that got her talking. She even looked at him as she spoke now. 'Oh yes, I know digging's necessary and all that; no hunt can persuade the farmers that it's a fox-control unit unless it accounts for a reasonable number each season . . . Well, few hunts can do that unless quite frequently, when foxes go to ground, the men get to work with their spades and the terriers are put down . . . and the humane killer is brought along, or the terrier bolts him and the hounds . . .'

'So what have you got against it?'

'What I think is that . . . well, for hounds to catch a fox in the open and kill him quick is fine and sporting, but to dig him when he finds an earth and has won the race and then put a fighter like say, Grizel, at his face when he's exhausted, that's callous.'

The breeze, coming up from the Channel, grew stronger and cloud shadows danced across the sheep pasture. Luke pursued his line. 'I suppose all Grizel's pups'll end up as working terriers?'

'No, not all.'

She fell thoughtfully silent again. She began wondering how those puppies would be disposed of. Doubtless one or two of them would end up as hunt terriers, taught to go to ground and harass and fight poor exhausted foxes that would, with superior cunning and speed, have outwitted, outstripped and eluded the mighty pack. The fact that the Owlhurst terriers were bred for that grisly task did not diminish her affection for them in the least. She just thought that if ever she owned one, for instance, one of her very own, it would never be allowed to be used out hunting, to 'go to ground' in that way. Its hunting life would be confined to rodents, rabbits and voles, squirrels and rats . . . Poor old Grizel, was she all right? Were those blind babies safe? Rose instinctively turned as though to return to the bicycles. She had to reassure herself.

'Lead on to the Firs, Rosie!' Jennings's shout came through the breeze over the backs of the hounds. 'I feel like a little extra today.'

She paused, then raised her whip in assent. The Firs would add another fifteen minutes on to hound exercise. She turned to Luke: 'Hope it won't make you late. I've forgotten what time your practice opens?'

'Oh, don't worry about me . . . By the way do you see much of Leonard Trench these days?'

'He calls me up quite a lot.' She answered casually, not adding that she thought Leonard Trench's invitations to drink, dine and dance were becoming rather overwhelming and journeys in his gold Aston Martin a little too nerve-racking.

'What do you think of him?' ventured Luke.

'Leonard? Oh, not bad company in small doses. What's your opinion, then?'

'To be frank I think he's flashy and a bit sly, too. Wouldn't trust him very far.'

Rose, who was well aware of Luke's jealousy, smiled at him. 'You're probably right.'

'Well, what do you really think?'

Rose gave a laugh that dismissed the subject: 'I think he looks smashing in his hunting pink! . . . But no, I'm not really an admirer.'

They'd reached the Firs and Jennings's voice carried to their backs: 'We'll be turning down to the bikes now!' he shouted. And in a moment they were heading north again and on the downward path that was flanked by church-spire tall chestnuts and beeches, dressed in springtime buds. She sensed the sap rising everywhere; the primroses would soon be over, the bluebells were thrusting through. The woodland smells were infinitely sweet to Rose, redolent, too, of young things everywhere, in nests, lairs, burrows and tree-trunk holes. And old Grizel, in time and in harmony with it all, had given birth that morning. Clever Grizel! Rose knew every hound and terrier at Owlhurst as well as she might have known her own children. but none belonged to her, nor to Jennings nor even to the Master. They were the property of the hunt, indirectly of the hunt subscribers, although the disposal of hunt terrier puppies, as well as foxhounds, had always been the prerogative of the Master.

'What are you thinking about?' Luke asked, when the stile where they had left the bikes was in sight.

'I was remembering a terrier I had when I was a child, a dog of my very own. He was called Jack.'

'What became of him?'

'When he was about five he got down a badger's sett and never came up again. He was the sweetest dog in the world. I cried for days. I was inconsolable for weeks.'

'Perhaps that's partly why you don't like terriers used out hunting?'

She did not answer. Luke saw that tears welled in her eyes at the memory of it — eyes that were far from him. But she was quickly recomposed.

At the top of the Old Shepherd's Way, the hounds were in every conceivable pose, a galaxy of brown, white and jet, squatting, scratching, standing, stern-waving, sniffing and panting, as they waited for their three guardians to get on the saddles of their bicycles and start peddling back to kennels.

'Are all Grizel's puppies booked, Ted?' She asked the question nonchalantly, unlocking her bicycle.

The old huntsman took off his cap and scratched at the

wispy grey on his dome. 'Ay, they's all goin'. Wanted soon as anyone knew she was in pup. There be only four like you've seen, and . . . well, pop'lar is Jack Russells.'

'Too popular by half,' put in Luke. 'You should see the number we vets are asked to put down by people who find them "too much of a handful".'

'All good homes, will they be?' asked Rose.

'All good — what?' he clapped his hand to his ear.

'Good homes!'

'Three of them's all right. Not sure about t'other.'

He named Mrs Wilson, the hunchback who rode side-saddle and young Mr and Mrs Dick Howard, followers of the adjacent Moakley Union hunt, who lived on the boundary of the two hunts and who had done several good turns for the Westdown. ' . . . and o'course we'll be keeping one of them, one of the dogs, that is, for Ben.'

'That's Ben Cooper, the terrier man.' Rose turned to Luke. 'Well then, who gets the fourth? she asked Jennings.

'Mr Leonard Trench.'

'Oh dear, oh dear,' said Luke, derision in his voice. 'Some mistake surely?'

'Well, like you, I was thinking he ain't the sort what oughter have a dog.'

Luke shook his head: 'Unsuitable in every way, that's my opinion.'

'I thought you'd say that!' Rose gave the vet another of her smiling admonitions.

'It's the little bitch he'd be getting, the runt of the litter. Even so maybe he didn't oughter . . . he do live in town they say.'

'That's right, Ted. He's a nine-to-fiver and Jack Russells aren't lap dogs.'

Rose hesitated. 'Well . . . yes, I suppose he shouldn't . . .'

'If you ask me,' said Luke, 'I'd put it a good deal more strongly than that.'

'The Major'll decide, he will.'

'That's right, Ted. So don't you think we ought to put it to Major Mayne — I mean that Leonard Trench shouldn't have a puppy — on the grounds that he's in London during the week.'

'Maybe I will an' all.'

'Or you could get Martin Eliot — the Master listens to Martin,' suggested Rose.

'Ay, I could. You likes our Mr Eliot, don't you, Rosie?'

'Yes, I do!' said Rose emphatically as she mounted her bicycle and began to lead hounds home without waiting for the other two. And Jennings looked a little embarrassed because he knew the last thing Luke Peterson wanted was to be reminded of 'Our Rosie's eye for that young Martin Eliot'.

Having seen the hounds in she went straight to the whelping-pen with another meal and bowls of milk. Grizel was looking quite content, but she was as hungry as a hunter. Rose picked up the puppies, one by one, and held them against her cheek. She raised the runt a second time, kissed it tenderly on the nose and drew a finger round the black markings that encircled its blind eyes and which ran from its black nose to its eyes, dividing the prominent white stripe of its blunt nose. Luke was standing next to her now.

'What a rude word "runt" is,' she said. 'Just because it's a bit smaller than its sister and brothers.'

'It certainly does look like being a weakling. But you never know how they'll fill out.' Luke glanced at his watch. 'Well, I must be off. Trust you to fall for the runt!' he added as he strode away.

'I love it . . . g'bye!' She thought about Luke's opinion of Leonard Trench — 'flashy and a bit sly, too' — and it began to dawn on her that, up to then, she'd been a little dazzled by Trench's opulence and sophisticated manner, his *savoir faire* and smooth patter, but really Luke was right. The glamour was full of chinks and holes and . . . no, this little mite she now held so tenderly in her hands *mustn't* be his.

'Ere, give us hand, Rosie! I gotter go 'n pick up flesh.'

A robust rather than a fragile beauty, Rose was large and strong and no lazybones either. By midday, having seen all the hounds into the grass yard, she had brought a new load of straw down from the loft, removed the soiled bedding and the droppings and put them on the dung heap, disinfected the courts, washed down the flesh hovel, mixed the feed, treated half a dozen injuries and brushed out the huntsman's office. Then she went home, which was just ten minutes' drive, and got her father's and her own lunch. When that was done she returned to help Ted feed the hounds, the fastidious eaters first, the gluttons last.

She knew each one by name and understood their foibles like a mother, and yet a firm, no-nonsense mother, who, if they fought too seriously, was quickly amongst them with a whip, shouting: 'Arr-h, break it up you lot! Get back Bracken, Lucifer. Down Craftsman or you'll be sorry, you will!' The only thing about foxhounds that really disturbed her was the callous way in which they were destroyed at the age of six or thereabouts. For them that was well into middle age. They'd be past their best; they'd lag in the hunting-field; and so they were shot. When that happened she'd make a point of being away from kennels.

At four that afternoon she and Jennings walked the hounds out a second time, taking the close route by the headlands round Renton's farm. After they returned and put the pack to bed Rose went to feed old Grizel again, then drove home to spend most of the evening tidying up for her father and preparing supper. By that time she had made a couple of resolutions about Grizel's puppies. She, Rose, would make a bid for the runt of the litter, and Leonard Trench would have none of them. She shrugged; these were probably nothing more than resolutions.

April 7

'I likes to see 'bout five inches left when they's grown up,' said Jennings in the process of docking the puppies' tails a few days after their birth. 'Nuff fer big bloke's fist to catch when they wants pullin' out of hole.'

Rose forced herself to watch, though she disapproved of docking. She turned to Martin Eliot, who was paying one of his frequent visits to Owlhurst. 'They ought to stay as nature intended, that's my view. This docking's just silly fashion.'

'Hunt terriers without cut tails,' muttered Jennings, ignoring both Rose's objection and the puppies' tiny cries of pain. 'Westdown hunt'd be the laughing stock o' the world.'

'It's barbaric,' Rose complained. 'But if it's necessary we should at least have had Luke here doing it.'

'Well, at least we don't take off the dew-claws as they do elsewhere,' put in Eliot, an angular loose-limbed man of thirty, a great lover of horses — and of hounds.

'Yes, that's a blessing, but, um . . .' Rose started, after Jennings had completed the grisly task.

'But, um — what?' asked Eliot.

'Well, I don't suppose you've been involved in the disposal of these puppies, but the Master's agreed to give one to Leonard Trench, and Ted and I don't think it's a good idea, because -.'

'Trench?' Eliot cut her in mid-sentence. 'He's not the right man to own a dog, certainly not a working breed. Lives alone, spends all day in a London office, moves down here weekends, back to London on Sundays. Besides which he's too much concerned with Mr Trench to look after a dog properly.'

'Well, I wasn't going to put it so strongly as that. But do you think we can do anything about it?'

Eliot paused, searching Rose's face intently. 'I'm damned sure we can. I'll have a word with John Mayne.'

'Oh, please do!'

April 8

In the middle of the afternoon, just before Jennings and Rose set out on hound exercise the following day, the old huntsman put his head round the office door with some welcome news.

'Had a 'phone call from the Master just then, Rosie. He says: "About them pups of Grizel's, Ted. You know as how I promised one to that Mr Trench." I do and all, I says. "Well," says he, "I gone and told Mr Trench as how I'd made a mistake like. I was expecting Grizel to have a litter of five or six like but as she only had but four there 'baint be none for him after all, Ted. I want you to find a good home for the fourth puppy, and not a word of what you done to Mr Trench, see? 'Cos he's that cut up, he thinks we done the dirty on him, which is true in a way though I know we done right." Very good, sir, says I.'

There was triumph written on Rose's face reflecting a flashing premonition that the runt was hers now.

'Oh, I am relieved. I bet that was Martin's work.'

'You been talking to him again, have you? Well now, Rosie, seeing you're so struck on Grizel's pups and in particular the little bitch, why don't you take it?'

'Oh Ted! Oh yes!'

'What you going to call her?'

'Gannet,' Rose replied beaming, and without hesitation.

'Gannet? Gannet? That ain't no name for a dorg. What you want to call it that for, eh?'

'A gannet's a big white sea-bird with black-tipped wings. My mother came from Lothian, close to the Bass Rock. We used to go on holidays up there and saw the gannets all the time. They've got distinctive black markings round their eyes just like that pup.'

'Can't be usual for a terrier. Ain't heard of the name in all my sixty-nine years. Well, whatever the name it's yours now, Rosie. But don't forget: *When pups is born on a stormy night, Life is going to be cruel and bitter. Life is going to be one long fight . . .*'.

'I know, I know,' laughed Rose, brushing her golden hair back from her cheeks, '*for the littlest one, the runt of the litter*'. If we believed all your old wives' tales, Ted, we'd be in a right state of gloom . . . Ah well, one thing I've got to be thankful for: Leonard Trench won't know it's my Gannet that was ear-marked for him.'

'I'm afraid that's where you're wrong,' replied the old huntsman. 'Our Mr Trench came round here day afore yesterday while you was home and he was looking for you and Martin to see his pup, and I showed them the litter and picked out the runt and I says: "That's yours, Mr Trench." I says "It's Rosie's favourite", and he seemed tickled pink when I tells him that. His face lit up like a bonfire and he says: "That'll be something for me and Rose to share." So he knows that one you're having was going to be his.'

'He does, does he? Well I hope that's not going to make any trouble.'

'That's Master's problem. It was him decided.'

'I wish,' said Rose, biting her lip, 'that I could be sure of that.'

April 12 — May 19

A week after the puppies' eyes opened, Rose began to wean them on cereal and milk. Ten days later, when they had ceased suckling altogether, she had them on meat, which she carefully selected from the flesh hovel, chopped very small, scraped, cooked and mixed with silk-sodden biscuit meal and fed four times a day. When they were not slumbering, they could be seen cavorting and fighting until they dropped and fell asleep. Gannet's appetite, like her build was appreciably smaller than that of her sister and two brothers and she still looked rather sickly. But she made up for this with her courage and defiant attitude and with her puppy bark which was more frequent and more fearsome than the others'. Being smaller and therefore increasingly on the defensive she relied more and more on those assets, and that made her the more aggressive, which in turn helped put on muscle and sinew and push apart her little cow hocks.

As the weeks passed Gannet grew more jealous, too. When she took possession of a stick or a piece of bone, even if she left it alone for a while, if one of the others was bold enough to try and pick it up, the runt's eye would open, and a growl would sound deep in her throat; she would circle round the impostor with a menacing look on her tiny and still rather blunt black-patterned face, until, having demoralized her opponent, she would go straight for its head and, with a yelp, it would run, tail-stump down, to a corner of the pen. On the odd occasion that Rose was there to witness such a dispute she giggled long and loud and began to love her puppy as she had never loved any other creature.

Leonard Trench asked her out twice during this period of Gannet's life, but, on both occasions, she found an excuse. She was rather mystified by the fact that he did not mention the puppy, especially since Martin Eliot had heard from the Master that Trench was very angry indeed at being refused, and knew quite well that Rose had got the one he'd been promised.

When the litter was seven weeks old, a few days after Luke Peterson had come along with his hard pad and distemper injections, Jennings removed the three that were going to outside homes to a separate pen in order to get them accustomed to being separated from Grizel, and during the second week in June Dick and Marjorie Howard collected the other bitch pup, which they named Candy. Mrs Wilson fetched Bob, as she called him, and Ben Cooper, the Westdown terrier man, came for Jimpy. When they left, Rose, who had not appreciated how fond she had become of them all, gave long wistful sighs. She had seen several litters into the world and had warmed to them all, but never as strongly as she warmed to Grizel's. She couldn't tell why; it was certainly not just because one of them was her very own. But she was happy about the fact that she was bound to see quite a lot of Candy, because the young Howards, although regular followers of the adjacent Moakley Union hunt, were close friends of hers and they promised that they would come over and exercise Candy with Gannet. And, of course, she would see plenty of Ben Cooper's Jimpy.

Predictably, the Western terrier man ('rough diamond with a loud voice, who always thinks he knows best,' as Rose described him), vowed with resounding triumph that he'd 'easily got the pick of the bunch'. Cooper, who was a gardener by profession, kept another couple of terriers at home. His intention was that his Jimpy should learn the ropes with those two, or, as he put it, 'be properly entered to fox'. When he came for Jimpy he annoyed Rose by giving a caustic chuckle and referring to Gannet as 'that little rat'.

'Going to make a worker of the little rat are you, Rosie?'

'No, I'm not, she'll just be mine.'

'Pity to mollycoddle a hunt terrier.'

'I assure you she'll not be "mollycoddled", Ben.'

The terrier man glanced in Grizel's pen and threw Gannet a snooty look. 'Bit deformed ain't she? Likely as not make a better lap-dog.'

'You wait and see,' answered Rose, 'she'll not be a lap-dog, either.'

* * *

Gannet, missing her playmates, became increasingly demanding of her dam, but Grizel having for the time being grown weary of childish play, afforded the runt less of her time. Not content with Rose's torn, knotted tights or Grizel's discarded bones or Jenning's old shoe, Gannet often ventured into the foxhounds' premises in search of a bit of fun. Some of the hounds disdained her, some bullied her until she raised her head, eyes closed and howled to the heavens; while others, leaning on their elbows, haunches up, lowered their heads to her level, inclined them impishly and played 'puppy' for ten minutes or so, while Gannet went into the attack, full of brave growls.

She made special friends with a veteran, a four-season doghound called Bountiful. Seeing this, Rose often drew Bountiful away from the others, out from the grass yard into the main yard to cavort with Gannet. But play came slowly. Bountiful would lie down in the sun, chin on forepaws, pretending to be asleep. Gannet would then prance up to him with her squeaking bark, snap at his muzzle, make a wild galloping circle, run at him again, fall over, wriggle quickly upright and then dash round him with little yelps, brow wrinkled, in a clearly challenging position.

At first Bountiful's only response to all this was to raise his majestic head, groan and lower it again on to his forepaws. Gannet pushed herself towards him on her belly, head on one side, jaws open, then collapsed with a yawn, emitting a plaintive sound that said: 'I'm bored, you *must* play.' Then, standing on her hind feet and crouching on her elbows and forepaws, she would bark again, and, very tentatively, paw his nose. At last Bountiful would raise one of his great pads, bring it down on Gannet's head and threateningly open his jaws. Thus the fun would commence. For Rose there was no better entertainment in the world.

But she had never known such a mischievous puppy. Gannet had an artful way of rejecting worming pills even when they were broken in small pieces, yet she always managed to wolf the meaty chunks of disguise that Rose rolled them in; it took all Luke Peterson's ingenuity to get worming pills down Gannet's throat. Weeks passed before Rose managed to stop her chasing Mrs Jennings's chickens, and it was months before she could train her to come to heel on the road.

Jennings never bothered much with regular exercise for those Westdown terriers that were kept at Owlhurst, but, by the time Gannet was three months old, hardly a day went by that Rose did not take her puppy and its dam for a regular hour's walk; for Rose, who rarely missed hound exercise, this meant three hours tramping or more a day. It amused her to see Gannet vanish down rabbit-holes behind Grizel, and sometimes, when Grizel scurried on to the next burrow, Gannet would fail to appear for what seemed an age, until at last the tiny, panting figure came scrambling out, all canine ecstasy, her red, black and white colouring besmirched with clay, her tongue lolling with lumps of it. She was soon leaping fences like a miniscule Grand National favourite. These long puppyhood romps helped to develop her lung room and depth through the heart. Soon she was putting almost as much muscle on her thighs as Grizel possessed, although in general appearance Gannet remained significantly smaller. To Rose's delight, too, Gannet developed a handsome rippling arch to her neck, while the black nose, with its pretty white-and-black marking, reaching up to and around the eyes, grew sharper by the week.

Although her coat remained short it thickened quite a lot at this stage and the unique red mottle on her back and sides became more prominent.

Within a few days of those first excursions Grizel caught a young rabbit and Gannet avidly licked the blood off her mother's muzzle; from that day forward hunting was her obsession. In October Grizel led Gannet down a fox's earth, and, to Rose's amazement, when they bolted a brace of cubs, it was Gannet, galloping at top speed, with legs outstretched like a rocking-horse, who was first behind them. She gave tongue up to halfway across the adjacent field. But Rose had mixed feelings about those young foxes being disturbed like that. Rabbits were different.

During those halcyon days Rose saw much of Martin Eliot; there was no one's company she enjoyed more than Martin's. Came the cubbing season Ted Jennings and Martin Eliot rode out in the early mornings, Wednesdays in the north country, Saturdays on the downs, while on other mornings Jennings and Rose, and usually Luke Peterson, continued their walking routine — reduced to half an hour now — with Grizel and Gannet scampering along with the best of them. Whenever there was a halt old Bountiful always left the pack to greet Gannet and give her a game.

When Trench called in at the kennels early in the New Year, Rose behaved coldly towards him and it was then that he referred to Gannet for the first time.

'You know that puppy of yours was promised to me?'

'No, I didn't,' said Rose, walking away.

'Well, it was and I think you should be grateful that I haven't made a fuss about it.'

'I know only one thing, that she was given to me and she's mine.'

With that, Rose, carrying Gannet, went smartly into the huntsman's office, leaving Leonard Trench alone and furious in the yard. She knew from that moment onward, she could never be on friendly terms with him again.

* * *

Dick and Marjorie Howard, the owners of Gannet's litter-sister, Candy, nearly always paid a Sunday afternoon visit to Owlhurst to accompany Rose, Grizel and Gannet on their walk. One afternoon in late February, four months after the start of hunting season, was to be a particularly memorable one for Gannet — for whom the presence that day of Luke Peterson, faithful as ever to Rose, was a fortunate chance.

There was a layer of snow on the landscape and the flakes were still falling light as swansdown. The two puppies, having filled out to adult proportions, were almost indistinguishable from Grizel as they gambolled across the white carpet, while the three of them raced back and forth, sometimes tumbling over one another, sometimes chasing each other in a catch-me-if-you-can game with the same abandoned delight that children display in snow; until, latching on to the alluring scent of rabbit, they gave the hedgerows their attention and, inspecting every warren, sped up and down, scattering the snow, like quicksilver in their terrier ballet.

During the past six months the ever inquisitive Gannet had managed to get herself stung by a wasp, prickled through the nose by a hedgehog, badly lamed from a festering thorn, hissed at by a snake, torn open on barbed wire, cornered and trampled by a herd of heifers and twice made sick by eating the flesh of long-dead animals. But at least those experiences had taught her to be rather more circumspect about awesome creatures and unfamiliar objects.

So when she came to the gin trap, concealed by snow except for its bait which lay tantalisingly on its square metal platform, she crouched and sniffed, creeping slowly towards it. Rose and the others were out of sight.

The bait, a piece of rabbit, held a special fascination for Gannet. Tentatively, with a cat-like gesture, she reached out as though to flick it off, mistrusting the contraption but determined to have its prize. The catch was set so finely, however, that no sooner did she touch it than the spring was released. Had she been one quarter of a second earlier in withdrawing her paw she would have escaped with impunity. As it was the jaws caught her very firmly by the two central claws of one of her forepaws and her sharp instantaneous cries of pain echoed through the trees of the big oak covert. In attempting to release herself she jerked her paw so violently that she ruptured the claws' tendons.

Rose ran to the spot as fast as she had run in her life, and kneeling, panting, beside her terrier, pulled the steel jaws apart and freed the anguished foot, while Gannet, notwithstanding her torment, tried to lick Rose's face with love and gratitude. When Luke reached the scene Rose wore a look of terrible dismay, for those two toes of Gannet's, bleeding profusely, hung limp by single threads of tendon. As though she could not bear to face the tragedy Rose glanced up for a moment, through the cold bare oak branches etched against the snow-filled sky, biting her lip. When she looked down again her expression had changed from alarm to anger.

Turning to Luke she let forth a diatribe against gamekeepers, and from gamekeepers she vented her wrath on members of syndicate shoots, the men who kept the gamekeepers in business, because she'd always been dead against game shooting, which, as she proclaimed with typical vehemence, was indulged in 'by a lot of silly rich pretentious people who haven't got the skill to make clean kills and for the most part aren't proper country folk anyway and couldn't care less about all the suffering caused by their horrid gamekeepers, pain and mutilation like this . . .'. In between her hissing sentences she soothed and comforted her beloved terrier, taking the scarf that Marjorie Howard offered and wrapping it tenderly round Gannet in her attempt to reduce the shivering.

With Rose next to him and Gannet well wrapped up and forever trying to lick her face, Luke drove straight to his surgery and severed the toes and dressed the foot there and then. Ten days passed before she was sound on that foot. The missing claws were to be her disfiguring hallmark forever.

CHAPTER TWO

'Just as well you don't want her to go to ground,' remarked Ben Cooper, holding the damaged foot that April and frowning. 'She wouldn't be much good 'avin' two claws short.'

'Nothing would please me more than your proving right,' Rose replied. For although she loved to see Gannet rabbit-hunting with Grizel, Rose never forgot her childhood pet, Jack, who got his foot caught by an oak root in a badger's sett and never came up again; her alarm, whenever Gannet stayed down for long, was acute.

'By the way, Ben,' she added, tongue-in-cheek, 'isn't it a shame that Jimpy hasn't turned out quite the way you expected.' Then she laughed at him, because it had caused a lot of amusement between Ted Jennings and herself that Gannet's brother, the much-vaunted Jimpy which Ben had taken as 'the best of the litter', though quite a keen rabbiter, had, to Ben's disgust, shown little interest in foxes. Ben grunted abstractedly, pretending that his thoughts were elsewhere, but he walked away with a grimace on his face and Rose laughed again.

After a couple of months Gannet showed the world that missing two toes made no apparent difference to her performance. She scratched and burrowed with as much relish and with as much effect as ever, and, to Rose's consternation, there was nothing the little terrier liked more than going to ground after fox.

Ben Cooper was out one day in June with his own terriers, together with Grizel and Gannet, when the so-called 'runt' drove a fox from its earth without any help from the others. Cooper was much impressed and, thereafter, whenever he went to the kennels and Rose was not in evidence he would mischievously encourage Gannet by shaking a fox's brush at her and generally prompting her natural aggressiveness.

Apple-faced Ben, by nature a taciturn man, was soon telling Rose: 'What a marvellous little hunt terrier your li'l Gannet'd make, the best in the country if I had charge of her. What a waste, eh?'

Rose gave him a mocking grin. 'Changed your tune a bit since last year, haven't you, Ben?'

'I have and all. Would never have believed that little rat'd fill out the way she has. She may be a small one, but, crikey, she's got guts and drive. She'll be ready for a spot of work next season . . . ah, come on, Rosie!'

'Over my dead body!'

August 14

As the year wore on, Gannet's reputation came to the ears of Leonard Trench who, up to that summer, still fancied his chances with Rose. The local speculation was that Trench, hearing that Gannet was, in a way, the first love of Rose's heart, thought he might still have an opportunity of winning that heart through the terrier. Putting on his most ingratiating smile and what he called his 'best country casuals' he drove his gold Aston Martin up to the kennels late one blazing August morning.

'Sorry to hear about that pup of ours getting its toes snapped off in a trap,' he said, stooping to catch Gannet, who quickly backed away with yaps of mistrust. 'Ah, well, teach the little devil to look where she's going in future.'

'What do you mean by "puppy of *ours*"?' demanded Rose, pausing in her work.

Still relying on what he called 'my charm' Trench followed terrier and mistress across the courtyard and into the kennels. His hand moved slowly to his breast pocket. Smirking, he took a cigarette, one of his Turkish specials, from its case, planted it in his holder and drew a lighter from the pocket of his immaculate twill trousers. 'As I mentioned before, she was due to go to me . . .'

'Well now, I just wonder why she *didn't* go to you?' Rose's tone was unmistakably sarcastic.

'No problem about that. I'll tell you. Out of the kindness of my little heart, I simply said to John Mayne — when I heard you had your eyes on it — "Oh go on, John, let Rose Maxwell have it, if it'll make her happy. Then she and I can share it," I said.'

'That's not by any means what we were told . . . And by the way, as you know quite well, we don't allow smoking in the kennels,' said Rose.

'Well, what *were* you told?' he asked, taking his lighted

cigarette from its holder, and stamping it underfoot with a mocking gesture.

'That you were not a suitable person to own a dog.' She was wondering why she had been foolish enough in the past to give Leonard Trench so much of her time. She had been only eighteen when she started going out with him — she had matured quite a lot since then. She had never despised him so much as she did facing him now in his brand-new twills and loud shirt, his polished brogues and his checked cap pulled down over his forehead, accentuating the haughty head-in-the-air image on his narrow white face. He always had looked so much more like a city shop-window advertisement for a 'country gent', she thought, than the real article.

That narrow face was now twitching with emotion. He went forward a couple of paces, putting it close to hers. 'You're not calling me a liar, are you?'

'I wouldn't be the first. I might call you a great many other things, too.' Having just seen the hounds from their grass yard into their lodging-rooms she was carrying a kennel whip. She was clutching the stock of it tightly and the whites of her knuckles stared at him.

Probably for the first time, Trench knew she had irrevocably rejected him. Prompted by jealousy and hurt pride his vindictive streak showed nakedly. He wanted revenge. Seeing that his words had rankled her he warmed to the duel. 'Well, I'll tell you what I think, Rose. I think you're a right minx. You know as well as I do that I had first refusal of that dog.'

'And I, like everyone else around here, reckon you'd give a dog a miserable life and therefore shouldn't be trusted with one.' It was so hot she felt she'd melt away. Little beads of perspiration had formed on her forehead. She wiped them away brusquely with her wrist.

'Oh you do, do you? Well I've a good mind to claim your Gannet back.'

'It'll do you no good, she's mine and that's that and the sooner you get out of here and make your mind up not to come back again the better.' Hardly able to control her voice, Rose headed for the kennels office, Gannet close to her heels.

Trench's petulant fury spilled right over. He threw his next riposte at her back. 'You're a cheat, that's what you are, Rose, a nasty cheat. What a long time it's taken me to wake up to that! I bet you talked John Mayne out of his first decision. I bet you turned on the charm.'

Trench was taking a sadistic pleasure in his taunts, while Rose's hand tightened on the stock of the whip she was carrying, his narrow eyes blazed. 'Yes, of course, you gave him the "come hither". I hear you're . . .'

'Get out of here,' she ordered, rounding on him and cracking the whip's thong on the flagstones between them. In the pause she heard the hounds' cries echoing through the kennels and Gannet yapping at the unwelcome visitor. Anger began to get the better of her.

He took a step nearer. 'I hear you're giving them all the glad-eye. Just because you're the best-looking bird for miles around you imagine that gives you the liberty to play the field. Everyone knows about you and Martin Eliot . . .'

It was Eliot's name that caused her to explode. She was so quick that he failed to cover his face when she delivered the first blow and the lash snaked round his cheek bringing up a crimson weal. Leonard Trench was no physical coward. But he was so shocked and bewildered by the attack that his cockiness suddenly vanished. He turned, stooping, arms raised protectively above his head. He was on the retreat. By no means finished Rose was swiftly behind him.

The next four strokes, delivered with all the fury in her heart and strength in her arm, whistled down on his back and across his neck. She heard him gasp. The fifth was an air shot, because by that time he was making fast across the yard for his Aston Martin, with Gannet, barking, close on his heels. Rose's last image of him that day was with Gannet's teeth in the hem of his trousers and him kicking her terrier away as he jumped into the car and started up. Breast heaving deeply, cheeks brightly flushed, still shaking from the whole episode, she threw the whip on to a pile of sacks. As Gannet came back to her, eyes adoring, tail-stump wagging frantically, a broad smile spread over Rose's face. She picked her terrier up and kissed her firmly between her big, limpid black-rimmed eyes. How she adored this little dog!

But Rose was not to know that, from that day forward, Trench would entirely blame 'the Gannet factor' for the failure of their relationship, and that he was to become absolutely dedicated to revenging himself on her through the terrier.

Invited by the Howards, Rose went to a Moakley Union hound show that September. It included a hunt terrier section for which she was determined to enter Gannet. But Ted persuaded her against it. 'You'd get her past a lot of judges, mind,' he had said, 'but they've got that Mr Derek Fowles judging at the Moakley Union, and 'e don't care for anythin' like missin' claws. E'd boot 'er straight out o' the ring, might even think you was insultin' 'im enterin' her.'

In fact, Fowles, a sallow, thin-lipped man of fifty, had admired Gannet at Owlhurst, and when he spotted Rose with her at the ringside he went over between classes for a chat. 'I see you've got that marvellous little Gannet with you. Pity about the claws, otherwise you could have won something here today.'

The unpleasant encounter with Leonard Trench was the last Rose saw of him until early in November when she attended one of her favourite Westdown events, the opening meet. Traditionally it was held close to the kennels, at the Queen of Spades, in the hamlet of Owlhurst. A good social occasion, she had thoroughly enjoyed it during her first year in her job and quite apart from that consideration, she knew Martin Eliot would be there. Her concern with Eliot was no longer all happy and positive, however, for she had seen him more than once with another girl since the start of the cubbing season. What with that and some scarcely veiled comments that had reached her ears, her misgivings had grown by the week.

Because Rose had told Luke Peterson she would be at the meet, he made a point of putting in an appearance, although, of course, he told everyone that he felt it was his responsibility as the Westdown's vet to see that all their animals, canine and equine, looked in blooming condition for the start of the season.

Luke had heard that the police had been tipped off that the Westdown was due for a visit from a contingent of the Hunt Saboteurs Association that morning and he was not only curious to know how they would play their hand, but, being Luke, a little anxious for Rose Maxwell's safety. The adjacent Moakley Union hunt, much of whose country was common land, was a more popular target for the anti-bloodsports people, but it was not unusual for the Westdown to attract the saboteurs once or twice a season.

As usual Eddy Jenkins, jovial landlord of the Queen of Spades and an old friend of the Westdown's, banned cars from his spacious gravel car park; so there was ample room for the twenty or so mounted and thirty foot followers who turned out on that special day. The twenty-one-and-a-half couple of hounds, accompanied by the Master and huntsman, Major Mayne, the kennel-huntsman and first whipper-in, Ted Jennings, and the amateur whip, Martin Eliot, all resplendent through the pale wintry mid-morning sunlight in velvet caps and brass-buttoned scarlet coats, lint-white breeches and mahogany-topped boots, looked a picture against the half-timbered pub with its playing-card portrait of Queen Anne swinging on a post.

Packing the car park, too, were the 'field', in relaxed chattering equestrian groups, a tight throng of well-groomed, plaited-maned horses, with equally well-groomed women and men astride them, wearing top hats, peaked velvet caps or bowler hats, shining boots and glinting spurs, red coats and black coats — all of which had been packed away in moth-balls during the past six close-season months. There were, too, at least a dozen children home from school, doing their best to control their ponies — Welsh, Connemara, New Forest and Exmoor — little bobbing, snorting creatures, not yet clipped and long of tail and mane, three or four of them wearing at the root of their tails the red ribbons of potential kickers. Gum-booted foot followers filtered between the horses' legs. The landlord and his family were handing round trays loaded with sausage rolls and pieces of cake, glasses of port and whisky.

Glancing towards the car park entrance, at about 10.30 Luke wondered if the saboteurs were really coming; the Westdown hadn't suffered from their actions as much as most hunts in the south. Luke imagined this was because John Mayne had insisted there would be no reaction to their tactics, that they would simply be ignored. 'Let the police take action for damage and the farmers for trespass; the rest of us should behave as though the "antis" weren't there. They get bored and lose interest if they're disdained,' Mayne always said. In the past the protesters had occasionally paraded their banners at Westdown meets and tried to distract the hounds — from their huntsman's commands by blowing horns and from the scent by spraying 'antimate'. But, as such behaviour proved fruitless with the Westdown and Mayne and his staff invariably managed to elude them, they usually chose some other hunt on which to vent their complaints, such as the adjacent Moakley Union.

Then Luke heard a policeman saying that seven or eight of them, students carrying banners, were now within a few minutes walk of the Queen of Spades, having parked their cars half a mile away. It looked like being a peaceful demonstration.

Luke spotted Gannet shivering nervously at the equestrian commotion, squatting close by Rose's feet. Every now and then the terrier put her forefeet on her mistress's knee and looked anxiously at her. The old doghound, Bountiful, separated himself from the pack and came across and exchanged a sniff with her. Inconsequentially, Luke worked out that Gannet was just seventeen months old. He could not forget that her birthday

had coincided with that happy April morning on the downs. Rose was talking to Dick and Marjorie Howard, who held Gannet's litter-sister, Candy, on a lead. Luke thought Rose looked sad, and wondered why. He joined them. 'Is Leonard Trench out?' he asked, remembering Rose's account of the drama at the kennels in August.

'Yes he is — over there.' The man whom Rose had rejected, very glossy in silk top hat, highly polished mahogany-topped boots, and impeccable scarlet swallow-tail coat, with an ingratiating smile and astride a big bay mare, was chatting to the rich old hunchback who rode side-saddle, Mrs Wilson, owner of one of Gannet's brothers. He was gulping a stirrup-cup, a glass of port. He lowered his string-gloved hand to the tray for another one, admiring the polished twinkle on the toe of his boot. The hand that held his reins also clutched his cigarette-holder from which his habitual Turk fumed close to his horse's mane.

'If I got my hands on him, I'd . . .' muttered Luke to himself.

Rose's attention was elsewhere. She was staring with set mouth and wistful eyes at Martin Eliot. He was in what seemed to Luke like intimate conversation with a beauty, Camilla Dewar, who was some eight years older than Rose. A newcomer to the Westdown at the start of the previous season, this girl had a reputation for being 'a bit of an equestrienne and for going very well to hounds'. It had also come to Luke's notice that Eliot was 'all over the girl', and he was well aware that Rose had heard the same news. Being an unselfish young man, Luke was not crowing; her regret, for whatever reason, made him sad, too.

But by this time, the attention of all those present, whether mounted or on foot, and although attempting to appear as though they hadn't noticed, was focusing on one thing and one thing only: the silent advent of the 'antis'.

Luke counted eight of them, grim-faced, slowly permeating the crowd's smart appearance with their anoraks and jeans and their crudely daubed placards: *Is it Kind to chase and kill Innocent Wild Animals? Put yourselves in the fox's place! Bloodsporters — Blood on Your Hands. Do some Soul-Searching, you Animal Murderers!* Eloquent banners — but silence from their bearers. The police officers, while keeping a careful eye on the intruders, made no move. The talk of the horsemen and women became less jocular, more contrived and stiff; many who would not normally have dreamed of taking more than one drink before hunting reached down nervously for second or third glasses. Those who carried trays for the publican rubbed shoulders with the protesters as though they did not see them.

Gannet, a good deal more sensitive than most dogs to changes in human mood and temperament, discerned the fraught atmosphere, pricked her ears, licked her muzzle and whined. Luke, divining the terrier's anxiety, stooped and scratched her behind the ear, and wished he could read the thoughts of the terrier's mistress. Gannet licked his fingers thankfully. Knowing Rose's ambivalent attitude towards hunting and her fair-mindedness he wondered how much of her sympathy lay with the demonstrators. Or was she totally preoccupied with Martin Eliot and the girl? He gazed at those two again: they were so involved they appeared oblivious of the situation.

Luke remembered afterwards checking his watch just then. It was 10.45 that the pandemonium began. Those eight placard-holders amounted to nothing more than a demonstrative feint, a diversionary advance-guard, dispatched by the saboteurs' leader to lull both police and huntsmen into thinking the rally was to be passive. Just five minutes after the placard-holders arrived, a dozen more saboteurs reached the car park by a footpath on the opposite side. Their arrival, which was heralded by horns and football rattles, was the signal for the placard-wielding youths and girls to warm up. They began shaking their slogan-banners, and, with the cacophony of the horn-blowing, shouting and rattling, it was as much as many of the equestrians could do to hold their mounts. Horses began rearing and plunging and neighing and three children on especially nervous ponies screamed for their parents' help.

The police sergeant standing with the hounds advised Mayne to lead the hunt off: the sooner the better. But by this stage in the riot that course was not immediately possible. Other saboteurs, comprising a second back-up party, had linked arms across the entrances to the car park. With rattles and yells of abuse, horns in high chorus and placards being swung this way and that, a current of panic swept through the scene of the Westdown's opening meet, not only through the fraternity of horses and riders and foot followers, but through the ranks of the saboteurs who realised that, with horses and ponies in a state of terror, they had created a very hazardous situation. It was during the ensuing few minutes' mayhem that Luke saved Gannet from serious injury, if not certain death.

Seeing Rose knocked sideways on the quarters of a pirouetting seventeen-hand chestnut, he dashed forward to help. Gannet pranced into the mêlée, barking indiscriminately at people and horses for all she was worth. The little terrier singled out Leonard Trench's voice, the voice she had grown to dislike intensely, shouting above the others, yelling with ugly invective at his mare to be still. Identifying that hated accent as being the source of all the trouble, Gannet ran close to Trench's mare, yapping and snapping within inches of the rounds of the horse's forefeet. The mare was already in a state of great fear and excitement and her neck was white with lather. Trench's vicious tugs on her mouth coupled with Gannet's urgent assaults were too much for the horse. Up she went on her hind legs, standing vertically and giving a long frightened whinny. With one desperate hand Trench clutched at her mane, while his cigarette and holder went flying. He clutched at the neckstrap with his other hand, but unable to keep his grip, he slid from the saddle, his behind thumping hard and painfully on the ground.

Despite the turbulence in the car park, Luke managed to catch and quieten the mare and lead her toward the prostrate Trench. But Trench, his face white, his mouth more twisted than ever in his rage, was concerned only with the offending Gannet who was snarling and snapping at a range of three feet, at the figure of the man she saw as her mistress's arch-enemy. But Rose had withdrawn with the Howards to a side door of the pub and everyone else was concerned with their own safety. Thus Luke was the only witness to Gannet's danger.

Trench was on his feet now, lame from the fall, the toe of one boot held painfully back against the ground. Gannet was the demon who had come between him and Rose; Gannet had caused his fall. He loathed this terrier. He would destroy her. He had retrieved his hunting whip and, scowling, was holding it in such a way as to use its bone handle as a bludgeon. Gannet, unaware of her peril, went in at him again, snarling. He brought the whip down with all his might towards her head, missed her by a hair's breadth, and broke the handle, four inches from its end, on the gravel ground. With the words 'You bloody little bitch, I'll kill you for that!' he raised his arm again.

Having handed the mare to a foot follower, Luke rushed to intervene. Gannet, still apparently careless of her real danger, stood her ground, drawing her lips above her teeth and snarling and snapping furiously. But now she felt Luke's hand under her; she felt herself whisked up and away. Trench's second venomous blow fell where, a second before, her head had been.

Trench vented his fury on Gannet's saviour. 'You interfering . . . I'll get you,' he fumed, hobbling towards Luke, whip raised. But something made him desist; he lowered his arm impotently. Looking up, he had noticed Major Mayne, who had maintained sang-froid throughout the riot, and was staring hard at him from his position by the hounds. Trench suddenly remembering himself, realised he was disgraced. He subsided and returned to his horse.

A few moments later, order was restored in the car park, and the demonstrators were seen off by the police. Major Mayne led hounds to the first draw. When the car park was clear, Luke, still shaken by the incident, gazed at the gravel for a moment or two, as though in a trance. He caught sight of Trench's cigarette still burning. He lifted his foot to stamp it out and as he did so he noticed its trade mark: Emir Hassan. Before the end of that hunting season he would have reason to take note of the inscription again.

In the knowledge that Mayne was a stickler for honourable behaviour and good conduct in the Westdown hunt, Luke telephoned him that evening to complain about Trench.

'I know all about it,' said Mayne, 'and I know all about his dealings with Rose, too. Don't worry: he'll receive a formal letter from me early next week telling him that he'll not in future be welcome at Westdown meets and that his name has been struck off the subscribers' list.'

'That,' said Luke, 'is the best news I've heard all day.'

Trench did not reply to Mayne's letter. But within a week he was riding with the adjacent Moakley Union hounds. Before Christmas Luke spotted him on foot — though not at the meet — on a Westdown day. 'Neither you nor I nor Gannet have seen the last of Mr Trench,' he told Rose, when he went to Owlhurst two or three days later. 'He's intent on revenge. I'm convinced of that.'

Rose was not happy. But Luke knew her sadness still had everything to do with Eliot, and nothing to do with Trench.

* * *

Hounds had been out from their mid-week meet and, served by 'a screaming scent', had enjoyed in mid-January the best day of the season so far, culminating with an evening hunt in which they had caught their fox in the open after a five-mile run. So next day hound exercise was confined to the grass yard. Rose took Grizel and Gannet out independently.

She was acquainted with every acre within a three-mile radius of Owlhurst. Her favourite destination when she was on her own was not the downs but a remote gravel quarry close to the perimeter of that radius. One end of the quarry consisted of a lake, nearly three acres in expanse, which attracted all manner of wildfowl, especially in mid-winter, while the dry end of the quarry was literally riddled with rabbit warrens. The surrounding willows even attracted some quite rare songbirds.

Rose's routine, when she visited this sanctuary was to conceal herself above the rim of it, between the wet end and the dry end, so that while she was immersed in the comings and goings of the wigeon and teal, the Canada geese, mallard, pintail and the waders, the terriers enjoyed themselves, too, weaving and snaking through the brambles and briars and in and out of the yellow-clay holes, until, after about fifteen minutes, every bobbing white scut in the colony was dismissed to ground. Then Rose would call Grizel and Gannet and the denizens of the warren would be left in peace until favoured with a fresh terrier visit.

Rose reached the quarry at about 2.45 that afternoon. Being more or less over the hump of her upset concerning Martin Eliot, she was almost back to her old cheerful self. She had become so keen on identifying the duck and geese that she was in the habit of taking with her binoculars and a pocket field guide of birds. Having learned to approach the lake with great caution it was not owing to any negligence on her part that she slipped as she stood near the edge of the cliff overlooking the dry part of the quarry.

Her weight caused a minor landslide. She careered down the nearly vertical slope, a distance of almost sixty feet, and would have broken every bone in her body, if not been killed outright, had her headlong tumble not been broken by thorn bushes. As it was she escaped with a fractured rib as she collided with her field-glasses, severe bruising and scratching and

— what was much worse, since it immobilised her — a broken ankle.

A hundred yards or more away Grizel continued her rabbit-yapping, but Gannet, hearing her mistress's moans and sensing at once that she was in serious trouble, was up at the place where she lay in a matter of seconds, circling around her, whimpering, nervously twitching her tail and licking Rose's face and hands for all she was worth.

Rose, hair askew across her scratched cheeks, attempted to stand on her sound foot. But conceding to the shooting spasms of pain, lowered herself with a gasp and muttered to her adoring terrier: 'No good love, it's no good.' No sooner had she recovered from the initial shock of her fall, and the agony of attempting to raise herself, than the full and dreadful knowledge of her situation dawned upon her. She was stuck in that lonely barren place with no help even remotely at hand. It would soon be dark — and getting colder by the hour. And even when morning came what on earth could she do? Her breathing became short because of the ache on her rib; she gave quick intakes of breath at each agonising spasm in her broken, swollen ankle.

Gannet, desperately wanting to help, wheeled round her, whining again and again. Suddenly, as though with the reasoning, calculating air of a human making a decision, she stopped stock still except for her panting, faced Rose and inclined her head with a quizzical look. Whereupon she trotted away up the pathway leading to the old vehicle entrance to the quarry, a determined little white figure, like a diminutive hospital nurse hurrying on an emergency errand. Rose, watching her departure, did not make a sound. She had no second thoughts about Gannet's destination. It would be Owlhurst. Without that conviction and despite the pain, she would undoubtedly have attempted to hop home.

A few minutes later Grizel was at Rose's side, looking very pleased with herself. She seemed to be as unconscious of Rose's plight as Gannet had been acutely aware of it. Rose's confidence waned a little now. Holding Grizel close to her against the cold, she was thinking — as well as she could think through the torment of her rib and ankle — that it would be one thing for Gannet to reach the kennels, quite another for her to persuade old Ted to come to the quarry. All of a sudden she felt faint. 'Oh Grizel, I think I'm going to pass out,' she whispered, and despite the descending frost, she did. All was quiet on the lake now; the waterfowl were resting. When Rose came round a quarter moon had risen in the fading sky.

Gannet went to the huntsman's office and the yards first and, finding no one there proceeded straight to Jennings's cottage. Deaf old Ted never heard the scratching and barking on his back door. Nor did Mrs Jennings who was busy in the kitchen with a whirring mixing machine. Gannet, knowing quite well they were in, kept up her racket for seven or eight minutes; and at last Mrs Jennings went to the door.

'Ted! Ted!' she shouted with the trumpet voice that most women with hard-of-hearing husbands acquire.

'What is it then?' Jennings came through from the sitting-room, puffing at his pipe.

'Rose's little Ganny,' she said, wiping her hands on a kitchen towel. 'All covered in clay and lookin' as though she's bin a few miles.'

'Little *who*?'

'Gannet!'

'Well, I never did,' said Ted. 'Where you bin, eh Gan?'

With great agitation Gannet put her feet against Jenning's knee, whined, described three quick circles on the cottage flagstones, pawed him again and walked away from the door a dozen paces, looking beseechingly back at him. Then she repeated the whole performance.

'What you doing of, Ganny, coming back without Rosie, eh?'

'Where'd Rosie have been?' Mrs Jennings wanted to know.

'Dunno. Best see what her dog knows,' replied Ted, watching Gannet touch him on the leg and start trotting away, stopping and returning again.

'She's trying to show you something, old man, that's a certainty.'

Gannet's message having dawned on Jennings, too, he picked up his cap, put his pipe in his pocket and was starting after her.

'Here, careful where you go love, it's getting dark.'

'I know it's getting dark. It's that troubles me. If anything's happened to Rosie ... Anyhow, I'm following Ganny.'

Mrs Jennings ran after him with a torch. 'Here, you'd best take this!'

Once she had the huntsman in train, Gannet gave her tail

two dozen wags of satisfaction and without further hesitation strutted along the paths and headlands leading to the quarry.

To Rose, whose distress was compounded of cold, pain and acute anxiety, twilight had never in all her life descended as rapidly as it did that afternoon. And twilight was soon last light. Holding Grizel close to her for warmth and pulling her duffel coat even tighter around her body, she shivered — and shivered again. By 5.30 she resigned herself to spending a freezing night in that place which hitherto she had regarded as enchanting and now looked upon, in the pale chilly moonlight, as being as bleak as the moonscape itself.

When salvation came it came abruptly. Like a bolt from the blue, Gannet flew at her, displacing Grizel, squealing like one gone mad, body all a-quiver, ecstatic tongue working nineteen to the dozen, eyes shining like bright pools in the dark; while, in the same moment, Ted's voice — 'Rosie? — Rosie!' broke the silence as the beam of his torch flashed across her legs. And while the old huntsman attempted to extract from his kennel-girl what her damage was, she gave 90 per cent of her attention to her terrier, her delight and her saviour, who an hour later was lying prone at her side on the stretcher and in the ambulance.

Nor, once Rose was tucked up in her hospital bed, was Gannet to be denied. Scurrying out of Jennings's arms, in a flash she occupied a place on Rose's pillow. And when the nurses remonstrated, Rose told them with some vehemence, still in a state of shock: 'this is *my* dog, yes Gannet, the dog that's saved me, possibly saved my life. Surely some dispensation . . . I mean, it wouldn't be kind to snatch her away from me,' she argued breathlessly, 'after all we've shared . . . and considering all her courage and devotion.'

The sister was adamant as the starch she wore. 'I'm afraid I must insist on the dog going,' she ordered.

'Our Rosie's not quite herself, you'll understand,' Jennings remarked. And to Rose: 'You'll not be allowed 'er.'

'Oh, Ted!'

'C'mon, she'll be safe enough with me,' said Ted, dragging Gannet from the pillow after five minutes arguing.

At last Rose surrendered — not ungracefully. 'Oh, all right. You'd best keep her in kennels with Grizel. Dad couldn't cope with her.'

'Ah — and what about your Dad? asked Jennings. 'Where does he come on the priority list?'

'Will you give him a call — tell him what's happened.'

''Course I will, but 'oo'll look after 'im?'

'He can cope for a few days on his own. I'll give Luke Peterson a ring, I'm sure he'll help.'

'You don't 'alf lean 'eavily on that bloke . . . Well, get mended soon, Rosie.'

Jennings held Gannet tight as he made for the door of the ward. But so intent was she on being united with Rose that, with one frantic bark, she struggled free, jumped from his arms to the floor and back on to the bed in three single movements. With a groan Jennings gathered her up again, holding her by the scruff with all the force that was left in his old arthritic fingers.

March 23

Major Mayne's cheeks billowed out like crimson sails before a nor'easter while the steam from his lathered horse rose round his muddied scarlet; and the notes of his hunting horn echoed over the meadows.

Gone to ground!

This fox had run, from find to earth, no more than half a mile. Major Mayne would not give it 'best'. Nor would he dispose of it with the humane killer. He had decided to bolt it: to put a terrier down the earth and force it to fly for its life. His hounds needed blood, blood they had 'fairly caught'. Major Mayne never dallied longer than necessary — at either the draw or the dig. He liked to keep the momentum of the sport going, and this was one cause for his popularity with the Westdown followers. Where was that terrier man? He put his horn to his lips again, and his cheeks billowed anew.

Terriers up, please! said his music.

There was another good reason why he couldn't give this fox 'best'. He had never heard the local poultrymen and sheep farmers complain so loudly of chicken and lamb stealing as they were just now. What was that report last week? Thirty hens one night, half a dozen lambs the next? If he didn't stop and destroy foxes that hounds had traced to ground, the farmers wouldn't be so keen, to say the least, on letting the hunt trample over their land. But this fox was 'jolly well going to give hounds another run', he muttered to himself. Where was that fellow Ben Cooper? He took another deep breath and blew.

Bring up the terriers!

Even hearing the horn for the third urgent time Ben, who was no respecter of persons, did not increase the pace of his gumboot stride as he made his way from his Land Rover in the direction of the call. The Master could be in as much of a hurry as he darn well liked. Major Mayne's concern was merely to entertain his horsey toffs, whereas so far as Ben was concerned, the business of hunting was 'killing the varmints'. There were two hours of daylight left: the fox could wait. So, with Grizel and Gannet on leads and a spade athwart his shoulder, Ben sauntered at his own sweet pace towards the call.

And — carefree — he grinned at remembering his last experience with Gannet. Rosie Maxwell was still in hospital two months after her accident. Nice girl, Rosie, very nice. The trouble with her was she didn't know what was good for her own terrier. She had this sporting Gannet, but wasn't prepared to give the poor little thing the life it was born for, which was, of course, to seek out foxes underground on a hunting day. So she'd said she didn't want her terrier to go to ground? Well, what the eye doesn't see . . . A week ago Ben had taken both terriers earthstopping at dawn on a hunting day. He had put them down a dozen burrows and more to ensure Reynard was not at home. Then he'd gone to work with his spade, blocking the entrances, so that at least at those places the varmints wouldn't find a refuge.

Five hours later, when the Westdown hounds had run a fox to ground, Ben blocked all the entrances bar one, put Grizel down to face him, and watched with great satisfaction as Gannet whined deliriously at her dam's yapping. When Major Mayne gave orders for the fox to be shot, Ben had dug down to the point of Grizel's yapping and pulled her out by the scruff of the neck. Then Ted Jennings had shot the fox through the brain. When the hunt had moved on Ben lifted out the dead animal and played it, with a crazy repertoire of grunts and growls, at Gannet's face. And when Gannet had responded with all the ferocity of a leopardess facing a gorilla, Ben, giving the belly laugh which he reserved for his terriers' antics, told her: 'It'll be your turn next, Gannet, you little fire-eater!'

The terrier call sounded again, but Ben did not hurry.

In his capacity as amateur whipper-in, Martin Eliot was

keeping hounds back some forty yards from the earth, so that when the time came for the fox to bolt it would have a decent head-start. The hounds — some of them whining in anticipation of having another go at their fox — were saturated with the wet loam of the bramble coverts, ditches and field through which they had coursed. Eliot was holding Ted Jennings's horse, too, while Jennings himself was busy at the earth, scrutinising its entrances, judging which ones should be blocked and occasionally glancing at his watch and looking around for Ben Cooper.

Farther along the headland, beyond the pack, stood the equestrian groups of the Westdown's mounted field, enveloped in their horses' steam. It had been a difficult stretch of country to negotiate. Despite the brevity of the hunt, the field Master had been obliged to guide his followers by a circuitous route. Now, having got warmed up with the chase they began to feel the perspiration chill on them, while the mud dried on their white breeches and scarlet and black coats. For the most part they were not interested in the killing of foxes, but only in the sport, the excitement that running foxes afforded. They might have echoed Sir Walter Raleigh's adage: 'It is not the quarry, but the chase that is the splendour of our days . . .'

This dig, like all digs, would be tedious. So, while they hoped Major Mayne would soon get things moving again, they chatted about their horses and their children, their farming, their holiday plans and their social life. At one moment the sound of the voice of old Mrs Wilson, looking comfortable in her side-saddle, could be heard a little above the rest, asking Camilla Dewar: 'Have you had any news of how that nice kennel-girl, Rose Maxwell, is getting on in hospital?' But Miss Dewar's thoughts were far away. 'I really don't know,' she answered abstractedly, gazing in the direction of Martin Eliot.

Close to the fox's earth stood a dozen foot followers, topped with deerstalkers, tweed caps and head scarves, who, by contrast — being as intrigued by the prospect of the dig as the horsemen and women were disdainful of it — looked eagerly towards the earth. Among them, wearing a waterproof shooting jacket and a brightly checked cap above his narrow, white face, was Leonard Trench. Nearly four months had gone by since he was debarred from riding with the Westdown as penalty for his behaviour toward Rose and his vicious attack on Gannet at the opening meet. Those among the mounted field who spotted him, naturally regarded him with scorn, literally looking down on him from their mounted position. But none of them paused to wonder why — considering he had been struck off their subscription list and was usually to be seen riding with the Moakley Union — he continued to put in appearances on foot with the Westdown.

For Trench had earned a reputation for wanting to be 'in' with everyone. It was essential for his self-esteem to be recognised. It was necessary for his social aspirations to be known by those who were influential locally, and indispensable to his ego to be on chatting terms with the more 'humble' folk. Aided by his ingratiating smile, smooth and confidential manner, he made a point of hobnobbing with all sorts, from poachers' daughters to magistrates, from tycoons to terrier men, whenever he got the chance.

'Hallo, there, Ben!' he called, as Cooper's rotund, red-faced figure ambled past him. He pointed to Gannet. 'I see you have Rose's terrier out.'

Cooper stopped for a moment, looked through Trench and grunted.

'Clever of you to get Rose's permission. She always swore she'd never let any terrier of hers be put to ground after a hunted fox . . . And how she dotes on that little dog!'

Cooper gave another grunt and walked on. As soon as the terrier man's back was turned, Trench's lips clenched; for beneath the cheerfulness he put on for the world, he felt as bitter as ever towards Rose and Gannet.

Cooper was greeted by Ted Jennings at the earth: ''Bout time you were here an' all, Ben!' Then Jennings gave the terriers a second look. ''Ere, what you doin' with Gannet again, eh? I told you last time Rosie didn't want her taken to a dig.'

'That so?' said Ben. 'Well all I know is this is the proper place for any good terrier to be on 'unting day, so 'ere she be.'

'Eh?' Jennings, not hearing, cupped his ear with his hand. 'It ain't fair takin' advantage of her bein' in hospital. She'll not be best pleased if she hears, I tell you. She's stuck on that terrier more'n a man loves a woman. But it's Grizel you'll be sending down, I dersay?'

Cooper grunted.

While, under the direction of Jennings, Cooper and another man with a spade blocked up two out of four of the earth's entrances, Grizel and Gannet whined and strained at their anchored leads, leg muscles taut, ears pricked, mouths panting with expectancy, brows puckered with anticipation.

'That,' said one of the two rather severe-looking middle-aged women who stood in front of Leonard Trench, 'is the prettiest little terrier I've seen in all my born days.'

'Which one d'you mean, Mrs Slater?' asked her companion.

'The smaller of the two, the bitch nearest. Don't suppose she'd win at the shows, mind — too small, too much colour on her — but with that dainty little head and them lovely markings and that coupling and air of quality I reckon she'd be worth a packet of money on the Jack Russell market.'

'You're right, just the sort your customers are looking for.'

'That's what I was thinkin'. If I was to breed from the likes of her . . .'

Trench, while keeping an eye on the activity at the earth inclined his head and ear towards this dialogue with increasing curiosity. Then he heard Mayne's command, 'All right, Ben, let's see what your terrier can do!', followed by Jennings's protest, 'Here, not Rosie's bitch!' But Cooper, having already removed Gannet's collar, was clutching her by the scruff in front of the entrance to the earth and the words were hardly out of Jennings's mouth before Ben released her.

The earth contained a number of sidetracks. But Gannet's nose told her precisely where the fox lay, and her nostrils quivered delicately as she worked her way through the labyrinth towards him. Cooper used to tell Rose that a hunt terrier that had been encouraged to chase rabbits would never lie up to fox. But Gannet proved him wrong.

Silent until she confronted her opponent, then she yapped at his mask, quite undaunted by the fact that it was more than twice the size of her own. He charged her three times in that black tunnel; but on each occasion, like some veteran swordsman parrying a duelling partner, she danced out of range, then leapt forward again, snapping at his deadly muzzle, at last forcing him to withdraw. Where the burrow widened the fox turned on his tracks, and a few seconds later the Westdown followers were treated to a dramatic sight.

The fox surfaced and flew across the grass like a russet arrow, with Gannet — dyed red-ochre by the clay of the burrow — hard at his brush and yapping wildly. She had not travelled more than fifty yards, however, before Martin Eliot cheered the impatient pack on to their quarry. Gannet was promptly bowled over in the rush. A couple of hounds who were last in the race were about to attack her, mistaking her, in her orange-clay disguise, for the fox, when Eliot and Mayne immediately cantered forward to whip them off. But there was no need for that. Gannet rounded on the hounds and sent them packing with their sterns close between their thighs. The scene drew a sharp chorus of laughter from all who saw it. The only one who witnessed it and did not laugh was Leonard Trench: he was still listening to the chatter of the two women next to him.

'Well did you see *that*? She's got a heart that little bitch, Mrs Slater, a heart to match her beauty.'

'She has and all. Pity she isn't mine, that's all I can say.'

Trench put his head between them. 'Er — forgive me, I could not help overhearing you,' he confided very softly.

'Oh, yes?' said Mrs Slater.

'Well, I thought you might like to know that little bitch belongs to me.'

Mrs Slater frowned towards his whisper. 'Can't hear you!'

'I was just saying that terrier's *mine*. I have to speak very quietly. As you see I lend her to the hunt . . . I'd be willing to sell her.'

'Oh, would you now, well I might be quite willing to buy her. How old is she, eh?'

'Nearly two.'

'How much?'

'We could settle that when I bring her over. If you'd like to give me your address . . .'

Mrs Slater felt in the pocket of her mackintosh and pulled out a card. Trench read the centre inscription — *Mrs Mavis Slater, Terrier Breeder.* The address was Moakley Union country. He gave a self-satisfied smile.

There was only one person at the Westdown that day for whom Mrs Slater's face struck a chord and who saw Trench talking to her, and that was Ted Jennings. There was not much his old huntsman's eyes missed, and there wasn't a breeder of terriers for miles around he hadn't encountered. But he couldn't quite put a name to this one at the moment.

March 28

Jennings scarcely heard the hounds or the terriers baying from his cottage. But when he was around the kennels he was not so deaf that he couldn't decipher every different intonation in their voices. Fear and joy, anguish and love, hunger and the excited hope of a day's hunting were but six of their many moods he was able to interpret. Dogs, for Jennings, expressed as many subtle emotions as any human.

When he entered the kennel yard a few days later the chant that caught his ear above the others came from the terrier pen. It was that of Grizel. It was a tortured howl mixing melancholy and fear in its plaintive note. But, as he strode towards the pen with his big jerky old man's steps, the mood changed from anxiety to relief. Grizel put her feet against the pen door and squealed and switched her tail like a clockwork toy, dancing round and round in small circles. But Jennings sensed that something had upset her and because the fox-hounds were quiet his instincts told him that whatever had been the cause of Grizel's anxiety was hers alone. And why, he was wondering as he reached for the door, was there no sound from Gannet?

'What is it, Griz? What's eatin' you then? Where's your daughter, eh?'

Was Gannet sick? He opened the door and glanced quickly around the exercise area and the beds. There was no sign of Gannet. Had he forgotten to lock her in? He hesitated. No, he was darned sure he'd put her to bed. He inspected the door latch and the structure of the pen. Everything was secure. 'Maybe that devil Ben Cooper's had her out again without asking,' he muttered to himself. 'But if he'd had Gannet, he'd have had Grizel, too. Aside of which there's no huntin' today nor yet tomorrer. So where's the little bitch gone to? Lor, if anythin' happens to her Rosie'll have a fit, she's that stuck on Gannet.' Perhaps he'd left her out after all? He stumped round the whole kennel area, but only once because now he remembered for sure locking her up. He went to the kennels office and telephoned Cooper. The terrier man's wife answered saying: 'Ben's gone to work, Ted . . . well, no, he hasn't been near Owlhurst since last weekend . . . Gannet missing? Well I never . . . I hates ter think what our Rosie's going to say if anything's happened to her.'

Could Rose herself have been to the kennels and taken her? Ted knew she was not due to be discharged from hospital until the next day, but he didn't put it past her to discharge herself on whim a day early. He rang the hospital. 'Miss Maxwell?' said the man at the desk. 'Rose Maxwell? No, she's still up in her ward.'

Ever since the day of Rose's accident, when Gannet had come to Jennings's cottage and led him down at dusk to where Rose lay in the quarry the old huntsman had respected that little terrier as he had never quite respected any other. He understood perfectly why Rose loved Gannet, and now he felt acutely responsible to her. The girl had entrusted him with her favourite and that favourite had gone missing while she was in his care. He couldn't bear to think of Rose's reaction if anything unpleasant happened to the terrier. As he stood over the telephone worrying, he picked up the receiver on impulse and dialled the number of 'a lad I know,' as he put it to himself, 'who'd do anything in the world for Rosie — that young vet.'

Showing just as much concern over the matter as Jennings himself had done Luke Peterson immediately called his surgery and told his receptionist he might be half an hour or more late that morning. Within twenty minutes he was pulling up in the outer courtyard at Owlhurst. Quietly business-like as ever he cross-questioned Jennings as to the circumstances in which he had locked up the terrier, then he examined the pen from top to bottom. It was terrible, this. No one who knew Rose well could think of her without Gannet or Gannet without Rose. Luke knew it would be like losing a sister, perhaps worse.

'Well, your guess is as good as mine,' he said at last. 'She's been stolen. Are you sure you didn't hear anything in the night or maybe early this morning?'

'You know me — hard of hearin'.'

'Who's going to break the news to Rose?'

'I wouldn't like to, she'll be cut up somethin' terrible.'

Luke's gentle grey eyes rested on the huntsman's face for a moment or two. 'I'll tell her,' he said.

'You mark my words, if Gannet's been stolen the little dog'll have her revenge on whoever's done it.'

'What makes you think that?'

'I feel it in my bones.'

Not only had Luke looked in for a chat with her father each evening as he promised Rose he would, but he had paid her several visits in hospital as well. He was due to see her again that evening and his heart sank at the thought of the tidings he must carry. As he walked pensively towards his car his attention was caught by a familiar-looking cigarette-end on the courtyard. He picked it up and turned it over between forefinger and thumb. 'Emir Hassan' he read for the second time. For a moment he re-lived that scene in the car park on the day of the opening meet, and remembered Trench's threat to Gannet: 'You bloody little bitch — I'll kill you for that!' Luke retraced his steps to the kennel yard and found Jennings letting the hounds into their grass yard.

'Just one other thing, before I go, have you seen Mr Trench lately — Leonard Trench?'

'Ay, I sees him out on foot at the dig by Renton's, Saturday.'

'So he's still around. By himself, was he?'

Jennings took off his cap and scratched his wispy pate. 'Well, now you mention it he did have comp'ny. He was havin' a talk with a woman by name of . . . Oh dear, can't remember, can't remember, but it was a terrier breeder . . . Moakley way. That's one thing I remember from Saturday. The other was Ben using Gannet at the dig. Young devil. I haven't got the nerve to tell Rosie that when she comes out. She'll have Ben's guts she will.'

Luke gave Jennings a double take. 'Oh, Gannet was at the dig, was she?'

'Ay, she bolted the fox an' all.'

'So Trench would have recognised her, seeing he gave Rose all that trouble about her.'

'He may, he may not. Don't see what difference that makes.'

'Oh, I was only wondering . . . Anyway, I'll call in at the police station and give them Gannet's description,' promised Luke.

'Reckon it's come to that.'

'Meanwhile, Ted, you try and remember the name of that woman.'

'I will,' said Ted scratching his scalp again. 'I'll try.'

Luke was in touch with Trench after work that evening. 'I thought, as you had an interest in Gannet, you might like to know that she's gone missing.'

'Er . . . Sorry about that. What do you think's happened?'

'I believe she's been stolen. I've told the police.'

Luke heard Trench's heavy breathing.

'Well, if I can be of any help . . .'

'Maybe you can and maybe you can't.'

'I hope Rose hasn't taken it too badly.'

'I'm sure she'll take it very badly indeed. I'm going round to see her now. Good-bye.' As Luke replaced the receiver he found himself staring at his knuckles; he was going to find that terrier if it was the last thing he did.

Lying in a hospital bed for the first time in her life Rose had considered the sorriest aspect of her situation not the strapping on her slowly healing chest, nor the plaster on her ankle, nor even her boredom, but rather her separation from Gannet. For she and her terrier had formed a symbiosis, they were almost part of each other. Luke understood this intuitively, but the knowledge scarcely prepared him for her reaction when he told her, as gently as possible, that Gannet was lost. She neither cried nor hid her face in her hands. But, sitting in an armchair, with an expression of acute distress and shock on her face, she quietly questioned him about the circumstances of Gannet's absence. Then, hobbling round her bedspace, she began packing her suitcase.

'But, Rose, they're not letting you out until tomorrow.'

'I'm leaving this evening to find my dog and neither you nor the hospital staff nor wild horses are going to stop me. Will you help me with my things?' she asked, closing her case and picking up her stick.

'Well, seeing it's obvious you're not to be argued with — yes.'

Within a few days word reached the ears of all who subscribed to or served the Westdown hunt, mounted followers, foot followers, grooms, blacksmiths and village folk. 'Rose Maxwell's lost Gannet . . . Oh that's terrible, terrible . . . Have you heard? That wonderful little terrier of Rose's has gone missing . . . What, the good-looker that did that bolt at Renton's t'other day? . . . Whatever next? It'll kill Rose if that bitch don't turn up.'

CHAPTER THREE

Gannet had been miserably incarcerated in Mrs Slater's kennels for a fortnight when her new mistress came in. The woman leaned over her with fat white hands devoid of affection, and, with a sharp push here and a brusque pull there, said through the cigarette that dangled from the corner of her lips: 'Come on nicely you have, Sue, time to take the marriage vows, that's what's in store for you my girl.' Gannet gave the woman a wistfully anxious look. She had learned to respond to 'Sue'. That was the name the young man who had sold her to Mrs Slater had given. 'I don't believe in changing a dog's name,' Mrs Slater had told him. She didn't even know the young man's name — or where he came from.

It was raining that morning and the earthen floor of the tiny space that passed for an exercise area was topped by half an inch of mud. Mrs Slater's terriers slept on piles of newspapers laid in five old tea chests which housed eight terriers at that time. The chests lay at the rear of the kennel cage, which was a single wire-mesh affair, a very rusty and dilapidated pen, in Mrs Slater's back yard. Here and there a rusty nail that held the wire to its wooden frame had worked loose. Excreta lay everywhere. Gannet's kennel-mates were all more or less in poor condition with dull, dirty coats and dry noses and showing signs of fleas. The kennels were pervaded, too, by an atmosphere of fear and frustration, and owing to close confinement, boredom and malnutrition, there was much snapping and snarling and other signs of irritation. Gannet, as a newcomer, felt the others' hostility at almost every moment. But because she was on heat her space was wired off from the others.

Mrs Slater, a widow, who was employed behind the counter of a grocery store five days a week, kept her terriers locked up in that kennel all day and night, except first thing each weekday morning when she put on their leads and led them down the lane and back for just ten minutes exercise — 'an emptier,' she called it. Even at weekends, being a lazy woman, she only walked them as far as the canal — which was not more than half a mile away — and back, taking them on leads, three or four at a time. For food, she limited them to a communal bowl of broken biscuit, soaked in water, and frequently forgot to fill their water-bowls.

She enjoyed a reputation among the less well informed locals of 'loving dogs' because she kept so many of them. But one or two shrewd neighbours who were real animal-lovers aired the opinion that, apart from the money her terriers earned her, Mrs Slater's satisfaction in dog-keeping sprang from a desire to own and command life and to dominate it. Until a few years before she had had a husband whom she had subdued and bullied unmercifully. At first she had bitterly resented his dying. But the terriers had filled the vacuum. Her more perceptive neighbours also took note of the fact that, with her eyes to the market, she always cared quite well by contrast for her pregnant bitches and puppies.

Mrs Slater was well aware what the majority of Jack Russell lovers were looking for. Not for them the pugnacious, short and bandy-legged, squat-faced, nearly-all-white look of the regular hunt terrier, but one with a much more refined conformation, with pretty printed chiselled features and pretty markings to go with them, one that owned the old-fashioned romantic air of a terrier portrait by Landseer. The fact that 'Sue' possessed those looks like no other bitch Mrs Slater had ever seen was one bonus; her having proved the worth of her breed in the face of fox — and thus having the sporty character that terrier owners also cherished — was another. The type was not that common.

Mrs Slater had paid the young man more than she could really afford. But if 'Sue' was fertile and would reproduce that type Mrs Slater knew quite well she could demand a high price for Sue's progeny. Mrs Slater bent and scratched her just above the base of the tail, whereupon Gannet raised her tail and curled it to one side. 'Oh yes, you're "standing",' muttered the woman, 'you're ready for it, you are.' But who, she asked herself, would 'Sue's' mate be? She took a close look at Badger, a heavy, handsome fellow with two black eye-patches. No, not Badger — too big. How about Mr Saunders's Bandit? A little bit on the coarse side? No, he wasn't. He'd do. Beggars can't be choosers. You'd search the world over to find the ideal mate for this one, Mrs Slater was thinking. Her white fingers pulled Gannet's ear. 'You'll love Bandit, you will, Sue. Doesn't half know his job.' Then she fingered Gannet's bare ribs. 'We'll have to fatten you up, little bitch, won't we?'

Had Mrs Slater been a sensitive owner she would have known — not only from Gannet's emaciated body but from her whole demeanour, if not just from the infinitely sorrowful look in her dark brown eyes — that she was in poor condition because she was pining for her old life. Had Mrs Slater known the truth it would have been that Gannet lived for one thing only: to be reunited with Rose Maxwell.

Gannet watched Mrs Slater pick her way out of the kennel's mud. She listened to her fastening the latch. Then she returned to her tea chest, lay down on her pile of newspapers, rested her muzzle on her forepaws, and with a deep sigh, joined the other terriers in gazing resignedly through the raindrops. All the colour had departed from her life.

Mrs Slater was on the telephone that evening to Dick Saunders, the owner of Bandit, a terrier that was quite well known both for rugged good looks and potency. Mr Saunders was in possession of an impressive pedigree for Bandit, one that was endorsed by the Jack Russell Club of Great Britain. Mrs Slater had sold more pups by Bandit than she could remember. 'Mr Saunders doesn't appreciate Bandit's real value, that's for sure,' she said to herself.

'That Mr Saunders, is it? Mrs Slater here. Got a bit of fun lined up for your Bandit again.'

'Oh yes, Mrs S. Which bitch is it?'

'None as you'd know. Got it just over a fortnight ago. Best looker I ever clapped eyes on.'

'Your property?'

'Of course it's my property. Paid good money for it and all.'

'No offence meant, Mrs S. . . . Have you counted the days?'

'You can take it from me it'll be ripe as a plum Saturday.'

'Okey doke, Bandit's ready for stud any time, so bring her round Saturday midday. But I'd better warn you, stud's fee's gone up to £30.'

'If ever there was highway robbery . . .'

'£30 or no Bandit.'

There was a pause. If that little bitch doesn't produce, Mrs Slater was thinking, I'll knock her on the head.

'I'll be there,' she said at last.

Gannet was experiencing this new emotion, this itch, this urge to mark her territory with her scent, to communicate as far and wide as she was able, to leave messages as a shipwreck survivor might put out beacons and other signals to tell come who may of her presence, or as a shopkeeper might advertise her wares around the town. But these promptings were only promptings; she could not know they were directed at the whole world of male dogs. She was also feeling irritable, prickly, having lost her pure health and being kept in such restricted close confinement, not to mention having the urge to hunt for her true owner. For Gannet to be in a world where human affection was absent was to be like a waterfowl pinioned in a desert.

When Mrs Slater came down the following Saturday morning she grabbed Gannet by the scruff and put her in the back of her musty old car. She drove her the three miles round to Dick Saunders's place, rang Saunders's bell, and put her down in his back yard with the expectant Bandit. Gannet started her low, ominous snarl, interspersed with light angry snaps, a solo that more than one fox in the Westdown country had learned to dread.

Bandit was entirely white except for one tan ear and one tan foot. He was a good deal larger than Gannet, broad across the chest, well developed in all the right places and the owner of a quality head. He was in prime condition. With his dark brown eyes brightening at the sight of the visiting bitch, he strolled towards her, stumpy tail erect and quivering, ears pricked like a fox, hackles up — not with aggression but excited anticipation. As he nosed around Gannet's quarters, she backed away, giving that low angry rumbling from the back of her throat, while in her eyes distrust, alarm and outrage were mixed. Who was this intruder her captor had thrust into her personal space, this cocky, chop-licking, posturing male? She did not like the smell of him — at first. She continued to growl and snap, but she never retreated. She just stood on the concrete, quivering.

Bandit, delight written on every fibre of his small taut body, whined and slavered on the yard that was so very much his ground. Sometimes he pawed it, as a bull facing the matador paws the sand. Suddenly, instinctively and despite conflicting warnings, Gannet wheeled her tail invitingly and Bandit mounted her. But as soon as he was up and ready, she skipped to one side, jolting him off. A try, try, and try again dance ensued, Bandit ever patient, Gannet ever offering, but ever ultimately declining. Their owners watched them for half an hour before giving up hope.

'Reckon she'll not be takin' him, Mrs S.'

'What, your Bandit, the great seducer?' taunted Mrs Slater.

'To be honest I didn't think she would. She don't look in the rosiest state of health to me.'

Mrs Slater gave Bandit's owner a sharply indignant eye. 'There's nothing wrong with Sue. It was almost ready for him, I could tell. Let me bring it down in the morning. It'll have Bandit next time.'

'Righty-o, in the morning, same time,' agreed Dick Saunders tapping the dead ash from his pipe and turning on his heel. 'Come on, Bandit, better luck tomorrow, old chap.'

April 17

Every half-hour or so that night Gannet hopped from her squalid hutch to whine at the kennel's mesh. Where was that white pushy male that looked like her own kind in the Westdown country, that alarmed, yet fascinated her?

The dawn came, lighting up her depressing prison. All eight terriers jumped to the wire in chorus line, yapping, answering the bark of a dog in the road. That dog, roaming free out there, always barked at that time in the morning. Mrs Slater's terriers must salute it. A small but welcome diversion. Gannet heard the rasping voice: 'Come here, Sue! Come here, you little devil!' and she felt the fat white hands. Sniffing the alien cigarette smell of the musty car, she feared the journey, and soon found herself next to Bandit again.

However anxious and unhappy she may have been, Gannet's innate courage saved her from being cowed. This enforced meeting did offer a a break from the dismal kennels. On second acquaintance she began to enjoy Bandit's company. Becoming more confident, she grew mesmerized, too: this peculiar-smelling dog was proving delightful. They stood close alongside one another, nose-to-tail at first, stiff sterns shaking, hackles up, tongues flicking, ears stiff as starch. After less than two minutes Gannet swivelled her tail to one side and allowed him to mount her without any objection. As he reached across her, her dark brown eye met his berry-brown, and they panted feverishly.

'It's a tie,' declared Mrs Slater.

'No doubt about it,' agreed Dick Saunders. Another three or four minutes passed before the terriers parted. 'No doubt about it,' he repeated. 'Well, that'll be £30 if you please.'

'Not unless she has pups, it won't,' said Mrs Slater taking a reluctant Gannet under her arm.

They left Bandit complaining at the sudden stop to his pleasure. 'Come on, Bandit, old feller,' called Mr Saunders. But Bandit stood there whining and watching the point where he saw Gannet leave for a full five minutes after Mrs Slater had driven away.

* * *

'Penny's dropped,' old Ted shouted above the howling of his hounds. 'Name's Slater.'

'Who's Penny, for God's sake, and who's Slater?' With a frown Rose brushed her hair behind her shoulder, and lowered her kennel fork as she turned towards him. Although her ankle was still bound up she had been back on light work in the kennels for a few days now. Rose, who had never been incapacitated like this before, betrayed the frustration at her slow-healing injuries combined with deep misery at the loss of her dog.

'Mrs Slater, Rosie — breeds terriers.'

'Well?'

'You remember as how I tells you and the vet I see that young Trench in company with a terrier breeder whose face I couldn't rightly put a name to when Ben took Gannet to the dig?'

Rose's expression changed abruptly to one of interest. The image of Gannet was never far from her mind's eye. Still, every day, she called her name around the woods and fields, and made local enquiries through everyone she could think of. 'Of course I remember; go on, Ted.'

'It's come back to me. I seen her mug at more hound and terrier shows than I remember. Not as how I can see it makes no difference just because that Mrs Slater was talking to young Trench that day — it don't mean to say she can tell us where your Gannet is.'

'Do you know where this lady lives?'

'Crow'urst, about twenty mile from here. In the Moakley

country. I'll tell you something, Gannet'll get her own back on whoever stole her. I feel it deep down.'

Smiling thoughtfully, Rose put aside her fork, picked up her walking stick and hobbled towards the office. 'I'm going to ring Luke,' she told him.

'Well done, Ted — his memory's not so bad as he makes out,' said Luke coming round in the lunch hour, very pleased — judging by the beaming look on his face — at this opportunity of being in Rose's company again. 'I reckon we've got to find this Mrs Slater, and soon.'

Rose, who was absorbed with Grizel scampering around her feet, shook her head. 'I just can't believe Leonard Trench would have done such a thing — come here in the night or early in the morning or whenever, pinch Gannet from her kennel and blatantly sell her.'

Luke searched her face and smiled with a hint of mockery. 'I can! The trouble with you is you see too much good in everyone. Trench is a jealous, spiteful devil, who feels very very bitter towards you. But, even if he stole her, I doubt we'll ever prove it.'

'If this Mrs Slater breeds Jack Russells you'd have thought she have so many to choose from she could do without one extra brood bitch.'

'You'd be surprised, Rose. You should hear the talk in my surgery. Terriers with the looks and character of Gannet are worth their weight in gold. My guess is that somehow or other Leonard Trench got to know the Slater woman had taken a fancy to her on that hunting day and decided to strike while the iron was hot.'

Rose gazed at him. 'Ooh, if that's so, I'll make sure everyone in the Westdown and the Moakley country and every other country for miles round knows about it!'

'And just suppose it isn't so? He'll have us up for defamation of character, if I know him.'

'Well, what if we visit this lady? If she paid Trench good money for Gannet, she's hardly likely to hand her over. If she really values her, my guess is that she'll make quite sure we don't get a glimpse of any of her terriers.' They were standing within sight of the terrier pens. Scratching Grizel on the neck, Rose looked wistfully towards the kennel. 'Gannet could well be on heat now,' she sighed.

Luke followed her gaze. 'We mustn't lose any time. I can't

manage today. Are you game to visit the woman with me tomorrow?'

'Of course I am. But it's a long shot, isn't it?'

'A very long shot.'

* * *

A little before dark that evening Bandit, renowned stud terrier, was missing. Dick Saunders, who went to lock him up for the night, called all around his cottage, looking here there and everywhere shouting and whistling was of no avail. 'Blighter's on one of his prowls, I dersay,' he told his wife as they prepared for bed. 'But don't you worry, dear, he'll be home for breakfast.'

Ever aware of the proximity of bitches in season Bandit's preoccupation since his morning experience was to be re-united with Gannet. His sleeping hours had been interjected with little unconscious squeals and contortions of delight. Gannet had come to him with Mrs Slater. Many bitches had been brought to him from Mrs Slater's. And Bandit knew precisely where they were kennelled. He would reach Gannet if it was the last thing he did. Soon after 7 o'clock he jumped from his kitchen blanket with an overwhelming urge to be reunited. Heart pumping, he skipped out of the kitchen door and across the fields in the direction of Mrs Slater's, which was only a couple of miles away as the crow flies, nothing to a Bandit with a Gannet at the end of the trail.

Tomorrow he would return, approach Mr Saunders with short, cringing steps, head subserviently lowered, eyes turned meekly upwards, tail tucked between his thighs, tongue flicking nervously around his muzzle. Then he'd roll over on his back close to his master's feet, stump shaking, muzzle sycophantic, in abject surrender. But now, as he trotted over the pastures and the ploughs, head and stern high, neck arched, eye a-gleaming, he was the very antithesis of the grovelling cur. The uninhibited noises of the night, — foxes barking, owls hooting, the riotous howling of the watchdogs at Mr Bell's farm — all helped to heighten his excitement.

He was no more than halfway across the last paddock before Mrs Slater's place when he first distinguished whiffs of Gannet on the breeze. The fact that his paramour was shut in and that the only apparent means of access was the tightly fastened latch on the kennel door, was neither here nor there to Bandit. Careering over the wicket gate, the back way into Mrs Slater's patch, he headed straight for the pen.

By the time Bandit made that leap Gannet was aware of his presence, too, not from the sound of his perky feet but from the smell of him, wafting ever so faintly from the fields, so unique a scent that it superseded the stench of her miserable kennel-mates. Ears pricked, whiskers bristling, she jumped from her rotting tea-box, and in paroxysms of delight put her forefeet against the prison wire. In a moment Bandit was there and they were facing one another through the rusty metal mesh; they whined with excitement, sterns erectly quivering. The kennel being roofless Bandit jumped up against the wire several times with his whole strength, but it was too high for him to clear. Meanwhile the other terriers set up such a cacophony of yapping that it must have been heard throughout the village.

Lights were switched on in the cottage, a curtain was pulled aside, a shaft of light fell on the kennels. Bandit, oblivious of the danger, but only concerned with reaching his mate, was scratching at the place where the wire was tacked to the wooden frame. Gannet heard the back door of the cottage being opened, she heard Mrs Slater's smoker's cough. 'Quick, quick!' Gannet's frenzied bark seemed to say. For she knew that the wrath of this virago, this new mistress she so much disliked, would descend at any moment — with the fury of the storm that had greeted her birth at Owlhurst two years ago — on the back of this bold outsider, whose company she so much craved.

Bandit's passionate teeth and claws left deep scratches on the woodwork. The nails that held the wire mesh to the worm-ridden wood were rustier than the wire itself. Suddenly his frenetic work loosened and extracted the nails. Up came the wire. Without any hesitation Gannet wriggled through the aperture. The other terriers' barking had reached a crescendo. Mrs Slater's feet scraped in the yard and her cracked commanding voice, 'Stop your bloody racket or I'll beat the daylights out of you!', burst upon the other terriers' chorus. Bandit was dashing for the wicket gate, Gannet hard on his heels. Torchlight beamed on the terriers. Mrs Slater thought they were both her own: 'Come back her, you bitches!' But the words were hardly out of her mouth before Bandit had led

Gannet clear of Mrs Slater's shabby little property and away into the night. They had made good their escape. Now they were true mates, belonging only to one another.

April 18

For the first few hours following Gannet's breakout, the two terriers revelling in one another's company, simply danced over the fields, plunging and rolling and running circles, and yet all the time progressing in the direction of Bandit's hunting-grounds. An hour or two before dawn they found a place well-known to him, deep in a thick-bottomed oak copse. There they curled up, close together as could be, and slept till dawn.

* * *

Mid-April! Coming in the wake of the past fortnight such a sudden invasion of Gannet's senses by all the sights and scents

of springtime, the birdsong, the spring corn and unfurling leaf, the fox cubs, and young rabbits, the sap rising in the bramble coverts sent her leaping in ecstasies of delight. She and Bandit darted along the hedgerows, happily weaving this way and that on their quarry. Gannet, who was quicker on the turn, was the first to catch a young rabbit, which she shared with Bandit. It was the only decent bit of meat she had tasted since she was taken from Owlhurst. And it was wonderful to be free after the confinement of Mrs Slater's hateful pen, to breathe unsullied air in the company of this marvellous companion.

Bandit always scratched at the entrances to the burrows or tried to tunnel in pursuit when he put rabbits to ground, whereas Gannet let them go and went in search of fresh game. She was not going to waste her time burrowing, an activity she knew to be fruitless. When Bandit chopped a full grown myxomatosis sufferer later in the morning, Gannet seemed determined to do better. Rabbits were only *faute de mieux* so far as Gannet herself was concerned. Her next encounter was to be with fox.

Some two hundred yards from the canal — the waterway to which Mrs Slater walked her terriers at weekends — they found a huge earth with several entrances. Bandit scampered around it gleefully, but without any particular interest. Gannet, on the other hand, pushed the black button of her nose around one entrance after the other, detecting badger here, vole there, rabbit here, squirrel there, but more pungently than everything prevailed the smell that set her adrenalin going faster than any other: fox. Gannet, who seemed to possess a powerful divining sense about foxes' earths, knew without hesitation, that Reynard was at home. Not for one moment could she resist the dangerous temptation of a closer inspection.

Quick as a flash she vanished inside. But after a couple of yards the ever-increasing strength of fox scent bade caution. The tunnel was scarcely broad enough for fox. This entrance to the earth must have been an old rabbit burrow, probably long discarded. About nine or ten feet down, where a twisted oak root cut across the corner, Gannet encountered a sharp turn in the tunnel. Here the diameter was so narrow that she was obliged to twist her body excruciatingly, and, as she rounded the bend, she gave a little whimper of pain. Within another few seconds' crawl the passage widened to fox dimensions. After another few feet she came quite abruptly face to face with a large dog-fox. The stench of him informed her he was male, the width between the bright circles of his eyes, which was all that she could see of him, told her that he was large.

A blend of fear and the hunting urges of race, which were so paramount in Gannet herself, flooded her whole being. Giving herself an ample two feet berth of the deadly jaws she set up the high-pierced yapping that gave notice to the world above ground that she was 'lying up to fox'. She edged forward slightly. His eyes were shining, unblinking silver orbs, in the almost black tunnel. He snarled, flicking his muzzle to one side, then to the other and snapping angrily towards the nose of this canine intruder. At length his incisors caught her on the lip, on which beads of blood began to form, dropping very slowly to form a little pool on the clay. She flew at him, and he retreated, but no more than a pace. There was a great deal of difference between this situation and facing a fox that had gone to ground, worn out from a hectic hunt, and with humans above, ready with spades to rescue her at the crucial moment — yes, all the dreadful difference in the world.

Hearing the alarm in his mate's cry, Bandit followed her down. But unable to negotiate that twist with the oak root at the sharp corner, he began digging and, in doing so, pulled down an avalanche of clay, which momentarily smothered him. He backed quickly away and started burrowing again. But he had pulled a large portion of the tunnel roof down, blocking the narrow turn completely. For Bandit Gannet's cry was now reduced to a faint echo.

On the other side of the earthfall Gannet's situation was extremely critical. The fox was inclining forwards, and Gannet, with two or three vicious bites on her muzzle was inching backwards. There seemed to be no possible escape. A minute or two more found her rump against the clay wall which Bandit had unwittingly pulled down. She pushed and wriggled her bottom vainly against the obstruction. She could retreat no further, nor could she turn. The fox was snarling and snapping an inch from her face. She was yapping her defiance. His breath mingled with hers in that stuffy claustrophobic tunnel. She felt her heart pounding against the clay. He was ready to kill her.

No one and nothing, it seemed, could save her, no men with spades, no Ted Jennings, no Ben Cooper . . . no Rose, never a glimpse of Rose again. Her back was arched like a strung bow, her feet were bunched as close as a cat's on a pole;

the fox had her by her ear now. It was bleeding fast. No human witness, if such were possible, would have held out any hope for her. Already she had weakened. For, although twelve hours in the open had brought the old moist shine back to her nose and her coat showed the beginnings of a glow again, the past two weeks of scant exercise and poor diet, of pining in unhealthy kennels, had taken their toll of her strength. Be that as it may, hunched up against the cruelly unyielding clay walls, Gannet was ready to go on fighting till the last breath in her body expired. Her adversary inched forward again.

* * *

As Gannet crouched at the fox's mercy in her dark subterranean corner, Rose and Luke were knocking at Mrs Slater's door.

Giving the two of them a quick suspicious glance, Mrs Slater took the photo to the light of her living-room window. 'Yes, it does seem uncommon like a little bitch I had called Sue — real good-looking . . .'

'You *had*?' Luke frowned.

'She went off last night, believe it or not . . . Still it might not be her. Lots of them seem a bit the same in a photo.'

Rose delved in her handbag. 'Here's a picture showing her other side.'

'M'm yes, unless she's got a spittin' image twin that's my Sue.' Mrs Slater nodded but continued to look disagreeable.

'If your Sue's the same as my Gannet, Mrs Slater, she was stolen.'

Mrs Slater blew a long stream of cigarette smoke towards her visitors and gave Rose a hard look. 'Now, don't you start that, I'm no dog stealer. I paid good money for Sue, too much really.'

'But you might have bought a stolen terrier without knowing.'

'Doubt it. Quite a pleasant young bloke he was brought her out here.'

'What did he look like?' asked Luke. 'Had you ever seen him before?'

Mrs Slater lit another cigarette and pouted. 'Oh, questions, questions! I'm not tellin' you. We have confidences in the terrier trade.'

Rose faced Mrs Slater squarely: 'My terrier was missing two toes on a forefoot.'

The Jack Russell breeder reddened as she paused to reply. 'That so? Well I didn't notice Sue's toes,' she lied.

If we identify her when she returns, we'll pay whatever you paid for her.'

'I don't know I want to do business with you, comin' here accusin' me of doin' deals with people that steal. Besides which I don't count on her comin' back seein' she's skedaddled with that little devil Bandit.'

'Oh, is it another of yours?' asked Luke good humouredly.

'No — neighbour of mine, name of Saunders. Sue was on heat, see. I had her mated yesterday with Bandit. Little monkey he is, but a good stud dog.'

'I see,' said Luke. 'I think we ought to go and visit this Mr Saunders. Would you very kindly let us have his number?'

'No, I won't,' replied Mrs Slater. 'I haven't liked your attitude, Mr Peterson, nor your friend's, ever since you come in here.' At which she crossed the room to her front door, opened it and ushered them out with a cold glassy stare and a final puff of cigarette smoke at their backs.

Rose and Luke made straight for the nearest telephone box and scoured the local directory for the name Saunders. Mrs Saunders answered the telephone. 'Maxwell, did you say? No, Mr Saunders is away today and tomorrow. Yes, that's right, our Bandit's got himself lost, not for the first time, neither . . . That's right, mated with a lovely little red-and-white bitch of that Mrs Slater's yesterday. Oh, that one's gone missing, too, has it? Little rascals, ain't they, eh? . . . All right then, Miss Maxwell, you come along with your friend and talk to my husband about it day after tomorrow . . .'

While Rose and Luke were speaking to Mrs Saunders, desperate, cornered Gannet took what was to be one of the most important actions of her chequered life. Soon after the fox bit her savagely through the ear, mustering every ounce of strength that was left in her small, weakened body, she threw herself at his face and caught him on the nose with a crunch of grizzle. He whimpered and backed away. But, in riposte, he closed his jaws so sharply over one of her pads that he exposed a tendon, and, from her toes to her elbow, Gannet felt a sudden numbness in that leg. The pain put her in a blazing fury. This anger, coupled with her urgent longing for life, drove her to the most fanatic aggression. Standing only on three legs now, with a series of wild yelps she snapped at his mask again and again. He seemed to be wearying, and, perhaps more from shock than from any other reaction, he retreated. Every time he withdrew she repeated her assaults, and at length he backed several yards to a wide place half flooded with the light of day.

This entrance to the earth was a seven-foot declivity that sloped down at a sharp angle from ground level to the small arena on which Gannet and the fox now stood, snarling at one another with blood-soaked faces, he so large with his russet spring coat and white-tagged brush, she so diminutive and clay-caked. Balanced on her three good legs she flew at him again, catching him with her needle teeth in the lip, and this time he turned and leaped up the side of the burrow shaft that led to the floor of the copse. In two bounds he was away. Gannet tried to jump after him, but with one foot useless she could secure no toehold. She fell over on her back. Even if she had been fresh and in possession of four sound legs, she would have been hard put to make the top.

Up against a wall of the earth she saw a pile of rabbit skin and bones, freshly left from a meal and eaten almost totally clean of flesh. That was what the fox had been busy with in this underground corner that was part of a large warren. She limped across and sniffed it. Acutely thirsty from the effort and the dust, she lay there panting for the next four hours with pools of blood forming in the clay below her foot and her head. She listened for sounds of Bandit. There were none. Her mate had scampered away in pursuit of the fox and then found other quarry to interest him. He seemed to have forgotten Gannet. She felt terribly alone.

Last night she had escaped from an infernal human gaol, now it was imperative to escape from a natural prison. The near vertical entrance above her was clearly impossible. Unthreatened and unencumbered by the fox she would reinvestigate the narrow tunnel whence she came. Sensation having returned to her bitten foot, which was throbbing with pain, she limped back to the point where Bandit had caused the blockage. She sniffed it and scratched at it with a single paw. She could make no impression on it whatever. Dismally, she went back to the spot illuminated by the daylight from the shaft through which her antagonist had fled. In the recesses of this lair were more clusters of fur and bone. She put her nostrils to them one by one. Did other foxes hide here to devour their kills? Would one of them soon be here again? She put her bone-dry clay-caked nose once more to each pile and gave a little shudder.

She looked up at the oak branches sixty feet and more above her. When the wingbeat of pigeons coming in to roost died down the branches were dimmed by twilight; soon they were enveloped in the blackness of the night, and the owls began to hoot. Up there was an April night in all its starlit magic, down here was nothing but little piles of rabbit skin and bones. She lowered her torn muzzle on to her bloody paw and groaned. She slept fitfully, her dreams alternating between mortal combat with a fox the size of a bear and golden visions of a happy kennels and a familiar countryside in springtime and a girl with whom she had formed what had once seemed to be the enduring bond of her life.

* * *

With the first hint of daylight came a sharp, anxious whining above her. Gannet looked up, abruptly alert, ears pricked. There was Bandit's white triangle of a face looking down at her with furrowed brows, agitated and enquiring. She barked at him and he barked back; but, although he described the whole circumference rim of the shaft and leaned into it several times with tail-shaking and much shrill squealing, he would not make the jump. A few seconds later he vanished.

April 20

For the next twenty-four hours Gannet merely nursed her woes. Her throat was parched with clay dust, her thirst was terrible. She was very hungry, too. She resigned herself to licking her injured foot, only stopping to lift her head and listen to some unusual noise in the copse above. The fox's bite had driven deep into the paw that was missing two toes from the keeper's trap. But after a few more hours it had mended a little, the pain subsided. She could stand on it now. She could use both fore-paws in conjunction.

Early afternoon found her staring at the opposite side of the lair, at the wall directly facing the narrow tunnel by which she had gained access. It looked soft. The instinct that sometimes tells the canine race where egress is possible, now prompted Gannet to scratch at that point, and, with a forgetfulness of her pains that was born of a desperate desire for freedom, she worked without pause. However increasingly starved and thirsty she felt, however confined and insecure, the more she dug, the greater the hope that sprang in her heart.

* * *

''Fraid you're out of luck,' Dick Saunders told Rose and Luke, his thumb stroking the silver stubble of his chin, the bowl of his dead old pipe clutched in his other hand. He was a tall lean man in his middle sixties with the sage honest eye of a true countryman. 'Bandit's been out three nights now. Probably romancin' with the one you reckon's yours. Funny, he's never been away so long as that before, although he's always been a great one for his prowls whenever there's an interestin' lady in the neighbourhood. Good little feller, really. Here, I'll show you his picture.' Saunders crossed to the mantelpiece, knocked his pipe ashes into a brass tray and picked up a couple of coloured photographs. 'Here he is with the missus . . .'

'Oh, I like the look of him,' smiled Rose, 'cheeky little face!'

'He's that all right!' agreed Mrs Saunders wiping her hands on her apron as she joined them from the kitchen. 'You see — he'll come crawlin' back any moment, all apologetic and "I won't do it again" in his eyes and rollin' on his back with his feet in the air.'

'And this is Gannet,' said Rose going to her handbag for the photos she had shown Mrs Slater.

Dick Saunders scrutinised the coloured prints Rose handed him, first one, then the other, then back to the first again. 'Ay . . . ay, that's the one Mrs Slater brought for Bandit three days ago. Small, but one of the best lookers I ever seen, that's allowing for the dirty state and poor physical condition Mrs Slater brought her in. Same with all hers.' Shaking his head at the thought of Mrs Slater, Saunders handed the photos to his wife.

'Are you quite certain it's her?' asked Luke.

'Bet my life on it!' Bandit's owner saw that a sadness had come into Rose's eyes and that she was biting her lip. 'Now then, don't you worry, my dear. Your Gannet wasn't in that bad a state or she wouldn't 've allowed Bandit to take her. Cheer up then. I expect they'll both come trottin' round the corner any mo' . . .' He reached for his pipe again and began to fill it. 'Mind you that Mrs Slater do keep her dogs in squalor. She's a mean old so-and-so. Her name's not all violets, least of all when it comes to dog keepin' and breedin', I can tell you. But I never heard she was a dog thief.'

'We think she bought Gannet from someone who stole her,' put in Luke. 'We're pretty certain who it was, too, only no way can we prove anything.'

Dick Saunders grunted. 'Well, I'll tell you something and I don't need to be much of a detective like to say it. Your bitch is on heat. Our Bandit's the greatest Don Juan for miles round, and he has her in the mornin', and they both go missin' the same night. Maybe you come to the same conclusion as me? They're together somewhere or other, eh?'

'Thank you, Mr Saunders,' said Luke. 'Will you be sure to let us know if your little Lothario turns up. Here's my card.'

'Okey doke.' Saunders was following them towards his garden gate now, and Rose, crestfallen, was gazing at his flagstoned path.

Then came a shout behind them. It was Mrs Saunders. 'Bandit's back! Bandit's back!' The three of them turned towards her as one. And they all laughed with relief to see the terrier squirming dejectedly on his back at Mrs Saunders's feet.

* * *

Gannet had been scratching at that soft face of the lair she had not chosen — the den from which she seemed to be determined to deliver herself if it was the last act of her life — on and off for close on five hours. She was about to give up the endeavour when she found she had made a little aperture, behind which was a hollowness. With fresh hope, working as fiercely as her wounded foot would allow, she created from that aperture a larger gap. Climbing over the pile of clay spoil she had made, she wriggled through it.

She found herself in a pipe, some two feet in diameter, and when she reacted to fresh shooting pains in her injured foot with a little squeal and a whimper, the echo of her cry came back to her as from a great distance. Anticipating another fox — for the tunnel did smell somewhat of fox — she started crawling the length of this disused man-made conduit with trepidation. She was now in pitch darkness. But, although she felt weak from the rigours and dramas of the past fifty hours, from pain and hunger and, above all, her terrible thirst, nothing would stop her life-or-death bid for freedom, not even the drifts of clay, one or two of which were piled almost to the top side of the pipeline. Once or twice she sniffed frantically here and there for a drink, but, although the cylinder was damp from end to end, there was not a lick of water to be had.

About two hundred yards from where she had started a tiny circle of light appeared in front of her. After another hundred yards the tunnel was faintly illuminated, and the glimmer soon became a glare. Reaching the end, her tired dust-rimmed eyes blinked at the spring sunbeams. The pipe debouched on to the bank of the same canal to which Mrs Slater had once walked Gannet and her other terriers on the restriction of leads.

It opened into a gutter which lay in a bank four feet wide. Gannet limped to the edge of the bank. There twenty feet below was the longed-for water. The cool waves twinkled and lapped tantalisingly at the embankment's water-line. Three feet above her was true ground level. The bank was moist and soft, but it offered her no puddle of water. Feeling the April sunlight on her grimy coat and thin ribs, a gentle weariness, stronger even than thirst or hunger or pain, came over her, and, after sniffing around the bank for a minute, she curled up, nose in hock, and receded into deep slumber.

* * *

'G'arn Bandit, you monkey!' urged Dick Saunders. 'Just you get on and show us where you bin and where your lady friend is, eh?' And with that injunction, the three of them, Saunders, with his pipe clenched between his teeth, Rose and Luke, stepped across the fields in the wake of the renowned stud terrier, the prodigal Bandit. He scampered more or less straight towards the big earth where he had last seen Gannet.

Ears pricked and boundlessly pleased with himself Bandit strutted, very business-like, from one entrance to the next, tail twitching, tongue lolling, then vanished down the rabbit-hole which Gannet had negotiated and he had inadvertently blocked up. He started digging at the earthfall once again.

Saunders, shrewd countryman that he was, put his ear close above the point where Bandit was scratching and whining. 'No doubt about it,' he said, 'this is the place that's been interestin' him these last couple of days. Deep . . .' he concluded, 'very deep.' Then, crossing to the declivity up which Gannet's fox had escaped, he reached down the length of it with his spade. Lowering himself with its support he peered all round the earth and in particular through the aperture by which Gannet had gained access to the drainpipe. Every now and then he called up to Rose and Luke — who were perched on the edge — with disjointed information: 'Remains of rabbit and chicken all over the place . . . foxes' eating-place, I shouldn't wonder . . . fresh diggin' . . . definitely dog scratchin'. Leads into a big drainage pipe, this hole . . .'

Saunders pushed his spade up towards Luke: 'Here, give us hand up, will you.' Kicking some narrow foot-rests into the side of the declivity, and with much puffing and blowing, he heaved himself to the entrance. 'Let's see if we can follow the drain to the canal, shall we?'

Saunders and Bandit were heading on through the copse now. Luke followed, but stopped and turned abruptly on hearing Rose's exclamation. 'Luke, see what I've found!' she was saying. She knelt at a place where the soil was damp. 'Here, look! It's an imprint of Gannet's foot, the one with the missing toes!'

In a moment the three of them were crouched gazing over the spot. Saunders broke the silence. 'What did I tell you? 'Course it was your bitch he had with him!'

* * *

'Mum! Mum! Look what I found then!' shouted Karen Bryant. 'Li'l doggie down here. It's got blood all over, it has.'

Gannet, stiff and tired, remained in her curled position, but lifted her torn face towards the child.

'Wait a mo', just coming, dearie,' said Mrs Bryant, an ample young woman with a careworn expression on her plump face, carrying a picnic basket. 'Where? What is it? . . . Oh, poor little mite. Let's fetch it up then. Don't touch it, Karen, or you'll dirty your skirt, and you never know what else you might pick up. Your auntie had a dog and it got fleas and worms and all sorts . . . Andy'll get it then. Andy? Andy? Where are you?'

Karen's brother, who at ten was two years younger than his sister, rushed up with a breathless, skipping motion. 'What is it, Mum?'

'Poor stray doggie's hurt. Just you climb down on to the bank and pick it up, there's a good lad. Here, take my mac and wrap it round or you might catch something horrible off of it.'

Badly lamed, with muzzle and ear darkened with dried blood, one eye swollen and half closed from a fox bite and a lip torn from another, Gannet did indeed present a miserable spectacle to the family. She gave a small squeal of shock when the boy knocked her bad foot. But she made no resistance. She welcomed the human presence. People meant bowls of food and water, people implied protection from all the hazards she'd just been through, people could be like Rose as well as Mrs Slater.

'It's in a horrible mess,' said Andy.

'Couldn't we take it home and wash it up, Mum?' suggested his sister.

'You have to be joking!'

'No, Mum, no, you talked about having a dog once, you did.'

'Well . . .'

'Oh, come on, Mum,' Karen added her enthusiasm. 'Let's take it home!'

'Would you really like it, kids?'

Andy skipped up and down, shaking Gannet in his arms and laughing. 'Oh, yes, we *would*.'

'Be careful, you'll frighten it! It's a friendly little mite, isn't it?' Mrs Bryant held out a finger for Gannet to lick.

'Dad'll love it,' said the boy.

'I'm not so sure about that.' They were standing by their car now, Mrs Bryant biting her lower lip, pondering. 'It's got no collar nor nothing, don't seem to belong to anyone particular . . . Oh, all right then. But it'll need a right proper bath.'

Quick as a flash Andy opened a rear door.

'No, not in there, Andy.' Mrs Bryant put out a restraining hand. 'If it comes, it goes in the boot. It'll be happy as anything there.'

In a moment the Bryants' car was crunching along the gravel of the towpath towards the main road leading northwards, and, in the boot, Gannet experienced a darkness more total even than the fox's earth, and a great deal more airless.

* * *

Bandit and Mr Saunders, Rose and Luke, soon reached the point where the drainage conduit opened out on to the gutter above the canal embankment, and Rose's heart gave another dip of despair not to find her terrier there.

'She might have got herself stuck in the pipe,' said Saunders.

'Or come out here,' Luke suggested, 'and wandered back to the copse.'

Rose cast an eye around the soft ground of the bank. 'I think I can see her footprints . . . Hold Bandit back, will you, Mr Saunders, or he'll tread them out. Yes, look, the missing toes again. Now we'll really find her!'

But they searched the area far and wide, calling and whistling vainly until twilight, when, having no torches, they picked their way slowly and carefully back to the Saunders's cottage.

Rose was as despondent as she had been the day Luke announced Gannet missing to her at the hospital. 'Do you think someone could have picked her up?' she asked Luke as he started to drive home.

'What in *that* short time?'

'It was just a thought. Anyhow I'll go out there and continue the search first thing in the morning. Dead or alive I'm going to find my dog, I swear I am.'

CHAPTER FOUR

'Hey, Mum, do you think it's OK in the boot?' Karen Bryant asked as the Ford met the A-road for London. 'I wouldn't like to go for a drive in our boot.'

'You're not a doggie, Karen; a doggie's a thing, not a person. It don't . . . well, it don't have feelings like us. It don't suffer the same. Anyhow, you know your Dad wouldn't have his precious seats dirtied. It had to go in the boot, didn't it? Made a right mess of me mac too. Hope it don't have a go at the picnic things.'

'What do you think Dad'll say?' Andy wanted to know.

'Go up in smoke likely as not. But he won't know till mid-morning, will he, he being on night shift.'

At first the smell of the picnic left-overs, which Mrs Bryant had securely covered, did remind Gannet very acutely of her hunger. Saliva kept rising in the glands of her mouth but rapidly dried up again for the lack of moisture in her body. Once she tried tearing at the basket with her teeth, but after a few minutes, locked in that small, black, airless place, she gave up the struggle. For hunger was by no means her first concern. The cap was loose on the spare petrol can which was wedged in a corner, and its fumes, coupled with the boot's airlessness, reduced her to a state of near suffocation. Now she was lying on her side investing all her energy into a desperate panting. Eye-lids stretched wide, her eyes stared into the blackness.

After half an hour they were well into the London suburbs. Although Gannet had never in her life heard such a roar of traffic, she was much too preoccupied with the fight to breathe for it to worry her. Had she not possessed a great deal more than the average dog's will-power and determination to live, she would probably have succumbed before the journey's end.

Mrs Bryant pulled the Ford up in front of 63a Plane Tree Road, Clapham. Gannet hardly noticed the boot being opened. She still lay on her side, eyes dilated, panting in quick short gasps.

'Oh, look at the poor mite!' exclaimed Mrs Bryant. 'Seems right tucked up, don't it?'

'D'you think it's ill, Mum?'

'It wants freshening up, that's what. Here you are, here's

the key, And'. Now up you go and fill a bucket of warm water. I'll be up in a sec' with the picnic things.'

The kitchen of the top-floor three-roomed tenement was very small. Gannet, still dazed and sick, crouched on the floor panting. But as soon as Andy turned on the tap she pricked her ears, head inclined. 'Look,' said Karen, 'Doggie's staring at the tap, isn't it funny?'

'Might want a drink of water.' Andy filled a bowl and placed it on the floor. Gannet dipped her muzzle into it and drank furiously. She didn't lift her head until the last drop had gone. It was her first drink since the morning she had romped with Bandit. Her body brightened visibly.

'Where does it go in that little body?' asked Karen.

'Pour out through her ears in a moment, I shouldn't wonder,' said her mother. 'Come on, you two, what about that bath?'

Karen and Andy enjoyed the dog-bath almost as much as Gannet ('Doggie' as she was now known) detested it. The soap-sting stayed in her eyes for two hours. For supper she got the picnic left-overs broken up and soaked in milk. She felt much better for that. They put down a blanket for her in the kitchen and all night she lay facing south. For instinct told her that south was where Rose and home were.

April 21

The next day at Owlhurst Ted Jennings, still full of sympathy, said he'd 'hold the fort' while Rose pursued her enquiries and her search. She called in at the local police station and the nearby animal shelter, but they all shook their heads. Hoping that Bandit might have picked up a clue she put in another visit to Dick Saunders. He advised her to 'have a chat with Mrs Slater'. Rose traced the woman to the shop where she worked, but, far from being in a mood for 'a chat', Mrs Slater was icily brusque. Joined later in the afternoon by Dick and Marjorie Howard and their dog, Candy, Rose continued her depressingly vain search in the areas of the canal bank and the fox's lair in the copse behind it.

Luke Peterson took her out to dinner that evening to cheer her up. 'Sorry I couldn't join you this afternoon. The surgery was overrun with overfed, under-exercised dog-owners and their overfed, under-exercised pets,' he said with his quiet humour. 'I reckon owners as well as dogs were suffering from heart and liver complaints. My only consolation is that I don't have to treat the owners.'

Rose was becoming very fond of Luke. He seemed to be the only person in the world who really understood why the loss of a 'mere terrier' should cause her such overwhelming sorrow. Her father and Jennings and Cooper and the Howards, while sympathetic, were really of the opinion that dogs were fairly expendable.

'You don't think I'm making a fool of myself, do you, Luke?'

'Far from it. Gannet went to fetch help for you when you were stuck in that cold quarry last winter and you know you have to return her faithfulness. Besides which you love the little thing, don't you?'

'Besides which I just know she's alive and I've a premonition I'm going to find her. She's out there somewhere — I'm sure of it — dreaming of Owlhurst.'

Luke raised his glass to her. 'We won't give up for quite a while, will we?'

'Well, I won't — not for a long time.'

* * *

That same morning had started early at Flat 4, 63a Plane Tree Road, Clapham, the Bryant children being very impatient to play with their new 'toy'.

'Here, let's take Doggie for walkies,' whispered Karen to Andy as soon as the first spring sunlight stole across their beds.

'That's a great idea. Where to?'

'Well, I was thinking, And', we could take it on the Common.'

Andy propped himself on his pillow looking doubtful. 'You know what Mum said last night. She said it'd get into trouble with other dogs and people on the Common and pick up diseases and get lost 'n' that.'

'I know,' said Karen with sudden inspiration. 'We'll tie a luggage label on its collar, that's what we'll do. Look, I'll take the label off the grip we 'ad when we were staying with Aunt Joan. I'll write "Doggie Bryant, 63 Plane Tree Road, Clapham".'

'Oh, you're a bright one, you are!'

'Where's my biro?'

'Here you are.'

Gannet started to her feet the moment she heard the children's footsteps at the kitchen door. She wagged her tail furiously when they tied the orange-coloured twine collar with the carefully inscribed luggage label on her neck, and then attached the twine length that would serve as a lead. For something told her that these preparations meant she would be taken out of this stuffy kitchen and perhaps have a chance to head home.

The smell of Clapham Common's grass was delightful in her nostrils, the first good whiff of grass she had had since that ecstatic morning with Bandit three days before. There were other dogs there, dogs off their leads, running, romping with gleeful abandon. A human was throwing a stick for his Alsatian to fetch, and when the dog carried it back and dropped it at the owner's feet, the man picked the stick up and threw it again. Gannet saw the Alsatian chase the stick in the same way that she once chased rabbits. She tugged at her crude lead. Except for the grassy smell all this was very unfamiliar.

'Now, let's let it off the string,' Karen suggested when they reached the middle of the Common. 'Look at the other dogs without leads, it's quite safe, I'm sure it is.'

'S'pose it's OK,' Andy agreed hesitantly, bending to undo the knot.

'Now, we'll see it playing and having a lovely time. Little thing deserves a break.'

For the sheer joy of galloping on grass and sensing the contrast of this freedom to the claustrophobic kitchen, Gannet went scampering in circles, nose to ground. As she raced, her nose wettened. Her urge to head south deserted her for the moment. She met a Boxer. They strutted towards one another, growling their challenge, hackles quivering, defensively enquiring. Having made friends, they chased one another's tails — until they were joined by an Airedale, and all three, in mad, paw-jerking rushes, played catch-as-catch-can. The owner of the Airedale, a young man dressed for jogging, laughed. He was laughing at the large and incongruous luggage label that Karen had tied to Gannet's twine collar.

'It's goin' a bit far, Karen.'

'That's all right, I heard they always come back to the hand what feeds them.'

'Oh, look, it's found one like itself!'

About a hundred yards away they saw Gannet nose to tail with a terrier of much the same general appearance as Bandit, only larger. It was white, except for black ears, one upright, one flopped, a black eye patch and a black tail. Wagging his stumpy tail furiously, this comic terrier put a forefoot on Gannet's shoulder and sniffed her ear. Then he lay on his back, nose between his forefeet, wriggling and looking delightedly at her from the corner of his eyes. Gannet obviously revelled in his company.

'Oh, ain't they a scream!' laughed Andy.

Gannet's new friend ran away from the children, Gannet with him. They moved side by side, playing skittishly, nipping each other on the neck, canine grins on their muzzles, affinity in their hearts.

'C'mon, Karen, they're out of sight!'

The children ran northwards across the Common, only stopping at the road. They looked this way and that, along the pavements and up the sides of the park. But there was no sign of Gannet.

'All dogs know the way home,' said Andy unconvincingly.

'And look,' added Karen, pointing to the twine she was carrying, 'I've got its lead, haven't I? It's sure to come to its lead, I heard they do.'

'If it don't get itself run over.'

'Oh, And', don't . . . what would Mum say? We'll get into horrible trouble for letting it off its lead.'

'Mum won't mind. She didn't want it that much, did she? Not really.'

'It'll come back, don't you mind. A copper or someone'll read my label with our address 'n' all.'

'We ought to look a bit further. Oh, I'd hate to lose it.'

'If I whistle it'll soon come,' promised Andy, rounding his lips.

* * *

The black-eared terrier led the way west down Clapham Common North Side, then to Lavender Hill and north-west by Latchmere Road. Gannet kept close to him on the inside of the pavement, two heads' length behind him, edging even closer when they crossed the road. So involved was she with this new companion that she entertained no other thought but to stay with him, to go wherever he went. For he was so like Bandit, promising perhaps the same joy that Bandit had given. People in north Clapham and Battersea stopped and smiled as the terriers pressed determinedly along the pavement, one a figure of fun in himself, the other rendered so by the luggage label that made her look like something destined for the post office. With all the resolution in the world the black-eared terrier pointed his muzzle for Battersea Bridge; Gannet never hesitated for one moment to follow him, and the Thames seemed to be twinkling and chuckling exclusively for the two of them.

At the end of the bridge, the black-eared dog turned right down to the Embankment, crossed the road via an island and so into the gardens of Cheyne Walk, whose trees were decked in pink-and-white blossom. On a bench close to the memorial plaque to Dante Gabriel Rossetti a tall bearded man lay nonchalantly on his back, his long legs crossed and relaxed, a wrist tucked behind his head as a pillow and a yachtsman's cap tipped over his eyes. He wore dark blue serge trousers and a thick dark blue pullover. His multi-coloured golfing umbrella was hooked on an arm of the seat. While Gannet squatted below, looking up in wonder, the black-eared terrier jumped on to the man's stomach. Showing no surprise the man pushed the sailor's cap from his eyes, but made no other movement.

'Well, well, Mountbatten, old chap,' he addressed the terrier in a quick whispering mutter, 'where've you been, eh? You are a roving roaming Jack Tar if ever there was one . . . aha, brought another friend with you, have you, always making new friends, aren't you? Hm, Jack Russell type, regular hunt working stock, I'll be bound. Nice looking little bitch, I'd say.' Holding Mountbatten by the scruff the man swung his long legs on to the path. Gannet took two steps forward and sniffed Mountbatten's master. His odour was the odour of many dogs. She felt his long-fingered hands lifting her.

'Hm, missing two claws, wonder how you did that?' he muttered, inspecting her all over. 'Well, what shall we call you, little bitch, eh? Here, let's have that silly bit of string off your neck, shall we? Much too tight — you look like a package that's on its way to Crufts,' he said, taking a penknife from his trouser pocket, snipping the twine and reading Karen Bryant's label.

'Clapham, eh? Something told me Mountbatten had gone south of the river. Well, one thing's certain, we'll not let you go back to Mr Bryant whoever he is, ought to be ashamed of himself. Crude writing . . . 'Doggie' indeed! What shall we call you?' he repeated, stroking his beard. 'I like your red markings, brighter than chestnut; be brighter still if you didn't have so many injuries, if you had a spot more condition in your little coat.'

The man's pedantic intonation did not suit his casual appearance. He stopped his murmuring monologue to let a couple pass. Then he returned to his prone position on the seat, and, this time with Gannet on his chest, continued without pause: 'Let's call her ''Red Ensign'', eh, Mountbatten, ''Reddy'' for short . . . no, no, W-R-N-S, yes, that's it, you'll be known as ''Little Wren''; never had a lady on board before, have we, Mountbatten? Let me introduce myself, Little Wren, I'm Jack Poynter, commonly known as ''Skipper''. Well, now, what we will do is this, we'll steer to Chelsea Gardens, pick up Bosun and the rest of the crew, then we'll steer for home. Have to see if we can keep you, Little Wren — may be overmanned,

you see, may not be able to afford an extra hand; George — that's the Bosun — and me aren't millionaires, just a couple of legacies and a little pension to live off.' Skipper sat up and clasped his hands behind his neck. Then he took some crusts from a paper bag and threw them to the ground. Four pigeons appeared as from nowhere, strutting towards the bread.

Gannet, having made firm friends with Mountbatten, gave every trusting and affectionate intimation that she liked Mountbatten's master, too. Now, with Mountbatten looking up at her, she felt herself lifted at arm's length, while Skipper started singing in a whisper, à la Gilbert and Sullivan:

Oh we're living off a pension from the Queen's nav-ee
And our sea-dogs share it, too, as you shall see-ee . . .

It was wonderfully comic scene: the bearded Skipper lying on his back, the peak of his cap now tilted over his ear, Gannet on his chest with a paw on his beard, Mountbatten between Skipper's knees, head carried to one side, and, below, the pigeons fighting for the crusts. It was a picture not to be wasted on one particular passer-by, a dark girl in sweater and jeans with a camera slung round her neck.

'Hold it!' shouted the girl.

Skipper frowned. 'Hold what?'

'Do you mind, it's such a fantastic picture. I'm practising, you see, I'm hoping to be a professional.'

'Yes, all right, why not?' said Skipper, reclining again.

The girl, delighted with the scene, went from this angle to that, taking half a dozen shots. By this time the pigeons had, despite the commotion, been joined by three more. With a quick 'thank you' the girl closed her camera case and walked on.

'Hey, wait a mo'.' called Skipper.

The photographer returned. 'Yes?'

'Be a good girl and send me a print, will you? I'll give you our address.' Skipper took a crumpled notebook and pencil from his hip pocket.

'Yes, of course,' agreed the girl.

Skipper licked the pencil lead two or three times, inscribed the details, tore out the page and, with great deliberation, handed it to the girl, and bade her goodbye. Then clutching Gannet, Skipper stood up to his six feet four inches, and with Mountbatten close on his heels, began to make his way towards Chelsea Gardens whistling *Hearts of Oak* and swinging his multi-coloured umbrella. 'Ah, there you are, Bosun!' he called, within moments of his arrival, to a stocky clean-shaven man of sixty, whose head as though possessing no neck seemed to be set directly on his shoulders. Like Skipper, Bosun wore a dark blue pullover and an old seaman's cap on which the sweat marks showed white. He, too, carried a large umbrella, whose panels were of several colours. 'Let me introduce you to an unaccompanied lady,' Skipper went on, holding Gannet towards his friend. 'Picked up, needless to say, by that roving old sea-dog, Mountbatten . . . I have called her Wren, Little Wren; rather cute, don't you think? Terrier — from *terra,* land, don't you know, adjective *terrarius.* Used for digging and following wild animals underground. A subterranean dog, Bosun.'

'She looks a bit worse for wear to me,' replied Bosun in his deep gravelly voice.

'A very shrewd observation, Bosun. Here, look at this,' continued Skipper, taking Karen Bryant's luggage label from his pocket. 'Had this tied to a piece of twine round her neck. You see — "Doggie Bryant, Clapham". Obviously hadn't the first idea how to look after her. Well, let's introduce her to the rest of the crew. Oh, look, they're all at sea.'

'I'll pipe them in,' offered Bosun, taking a whistle from his pocket and blowing it with apple-billowy cheeks. Five dogs came bounding across the grass, one perhaps a cross between a St Bernard and a collie, one with the appearance of a long-haired Dalmatian, three nondescript rough-coated toy-dog types and a black, shaggy creature with wild roving eyes. The five mongrels immediately set to work examining Gannet — and Mountbatten, too, for he'd obviously been somewhere foreign and exciting. Skipper introduced them.

'Little Wren, these are your temporary shipmates, Jellicoe, Nelson, Grenville, Beatty and Drake. Mountbatten you know already. We have one more you shall meet, too, a very, very old sea-dog called Collingwood, too old to go more than a few yards, poor dear. Right, Bosun, let's steer back to port. I'll carry Little Wren, you put the leads on the others.'

'Ay, Skipper, but we're not keeping that wee bitch, are we? I mean we've never taken on a Jill Tar before.'

'That's to be decided. We'll put it to the crew's vote when we get back.'

It was a sparse and spartan, if spacious bedsitter, with one large room and a kitchen and a bathroom. There was a double bunk for the men, one bed atop the other, with, on the floor immediately alongside the bunks, seven blankets for the dogs, set precisely the same distance apart, and neatly folded. On one blanket lay an ancient red setter, very thin, with oyster eyes, obvious signs of arthritis in all four feet and shivering despite the fact that he wore a knitted wool coat. His whole frame spoke volumes of misery. A table standing against the far wall carried a dozen books by Warren Tute, C.S. Forester, Nicholas Monsarrat and Alexander Kent. Above it was the flat's single picture — a print of Nelson's flagship, *Victory*.

'A bed for Little Wren . . . ah, *there* we are.' Skipper turned from Gannet to the dilapidated setter. 'Now, Little Wren — let me introduce you to poor old Collingwood.'

Bosun went to the cupboard, took out a blanket, folded it meticulously, and laid it equidistantly from the other seven. A little later he fetched eight bowls and set them down, like sailors on parade, one in front of each blanket. Whereupon Skipper who had mixed the basin of food, began ladling it out in such precisely equal shares (regardless of the respective sizes of the dogs) that it looked as though, if each share were weighed, there would not be an ounce between them.

Bosun swivelled his football head on his chunky square shoulders. 'Sit!' he ordered as Gannet and Drake lurched forward, chop-licking.

'All right,' said Skipper, after another minute, 'give the word!'

'Feed away!' shouted Bosun, and, Gannet, in unison with the others set her sights on a bowl and scampered forward. They all allowed 'poor old Collingwood' to eat without interference. Jellicoe and Nelson made an angry growling dash at Gannet, but Mountbatten, her self-appointed protector, intervened bravely and saw them off. Gannet, with a quick look of gratitude in her eyes and tail-shake of thanks, tucked in. It was the first really square and wholesome meal she'd had since Owlhurst. It sparked off vague and remote memories of Rose and the old life.

'Bacon and eggs do you, Skipper?'

'Oh, wonderful, Bosun!'

As for the dogs only Gannet, whose meal had reminded

her what real food was, ventured to ask for more. She placed a soliciting paw on Skipper's leg, accompanied by a small, hungry whine. Jellicoe, the rough-coated Dalmatian-type, growled furiously at her; Mountbatten, ever protective, placed himself between Jellicoe and Gannet.

Skipper raised a finger, telling them to be quiet. 'Can we or can we not afford a new crew member?' he asked Bosun. 'When did we last take in a stray?'

Bosun reminded him how they'd collected the one called Beatty from behind Chelsea Barracks last December, and that was to replace Raleigh who was run over by what Bosun described as an 'imbecile pilot' in Parliament Square. Bosun didn't think they were justified in taking on a new ship-mate. Skipper demurred. Bosun was of the opinion that it might be possible — 'If we have poor old Collingwood put down . . . It would be a great kindness, one shot of the needle — he'd know nothing.' Skipper reminded his mate that they'd agreed not to raise the sensitive subject of Collingwood. Finally Bosun quoted a 'ship's regulation', saying that bitches were definitely taboo in their apartment.

Skipper, memory suddenly jolted, tugged at his beard and gazed hard at Gannet. 'Yes, of course. We are becoming forgetful in our old age, aren't we? What would happen, Little Wren when you come into, er, an interesting condition. There might be a mutiny, no? Well, that's settled that one. So what about alternative accommodation?'

Bosun shook his head regretfully. 'I'm sure we all agree that Battersea's the only answer.'

Skipper turned his eyes reflectively at the ceiling for a moment, then focused them on Gannet again. 'Battersea,' he put his finger-tips together, intoning with great respect, 'the oldest canine shelter in the world, founded by Mrs Tealby in 1860, moved to Battersea in 1871, a good sanctuary, to which Bosun and I have delivered many lost friends. How many is it, Bosun? Well, never mind . . . Right, that settles it, Little Wren, you will rest your little head here tonight. After breakfast you will join us for our outing in the park. In the afternoon you will be offered to Battersea Dogs' Home. After that, Little Wren, God help you; given a fair wind and good fortune some kind soul may take you on his strength, otherwise . . .'

With a nasty squelching noise in his mouth, Skipper drew his forefinger sharply across his throat. 'Come on, Bosun, we'll have a quick cruise before dark, shall we? Got a spare collar and lead for Little Wren?'

Twenty minutes later each dog was obediently curled up on his appointed blanket, Mountbatten being at one end, next to Gannet. At about midnight he got up and licked her very tenderly on the ear for a few seconds. When he returned to his own blanket he lay watching her for a long time, as if to make sure she was safe.

The men noticed that Gannet whimpered in her sleep. Bosun put down Alexander Kent's *Success to the Brave,* for which Karen Bryant's luggage label had become a marker. 'Nightmare, I suppose — about her time with the Bryants,' he said.

'I don't think it's a miserable noise,' surmised Skipper, 'she might be dreaming of idyllic times from her puppyhood. Perhaps she was once a very happy little dog.'

'We'll never know, will we? Your turn to read, Skipper.'

Had Gannet been a human, had she registered the old huntsman's prophecy at her birth, had she understood what Skipper and Bosun had in mind for her, she would probably have stayed awake all night with insomnious dread in her heart, harbouring a ghastly fear for her future; but since she was only an animal, without the gift of understanding of human tongues, without reason, without intellect, she slept peacefully at Mountbatten's side, as though sure in her heart that she and he would never be parted.

* * *

With another bright day dawning over Millbank the 'ship's company', with the exception of old Collingwood, set off, as they were wont to do at least once a week, in the direction of Buckingham Palace to watch the Changing of the Guard. It was to prove a red-letter day for Skipper and Bosun. They walked via St James's Park, where Gannet stood statue-still for nearly a minute, enchanted by the flutter of wings on and above the water and the honking of the geese, which perhaps sparked off an image of the lake where Rose had watched for wildfowl. Arriving early at the Palace, the party secured a good vantage point. The sentries were being posted, the scarlet guardsmen wheeled and counter-marched to the sound of their brass and pipes and drums. A black Daimler carrying the Royal Standard purred out of the gates. Both men raised their hands to their caps in naval salutes, smiling broadly.

Skipper told Gannet: 'You're the luckiest dog alive. We've been coming here every week for twenty years and have only seen Her Majesty twice, That's right, isn't it, Bosun?'

The party circled across Green Park, took the subway below Hyde Park Corner and entered Hyde Park by the Achilles statue. The men visited the public lavatory, each holding all the dogs while the other 'pumped ship', as they put it. The dogs were let off their leads and fanned out across the grass, noses to the ground, like harriers sent to draw, Gannet with her country-bred sharpness ahead of them all. Not more than thirty yards from the shore of the Serpentine, Jellicoe, the one with the appearance of a long-haired Dalmatian, defecated within inches of the feet of an elderly woman who had dozed off on a bench. When she woke, less than a minute later, Jellicoe had moved on, and, by chance, Gannet was at the spot.

'Oh, you dirty little rascal,' the woman screamed, snatching up her umbrella and striking a blow at Gannet's back. But Gannet, shying away, was much too quick for her.

Skipper, seeing the incident, was promptly on the scene. He raised his sailor's cap and swung it, with a debonair flourish, to his knees. 'Madam, would you strike a poor defenceless little dog?'

The woman shifted her position to the end of the seat, gave Gannet a look of utter disgust, pointed with her umbrella at Jellicoe's message and upbraided Skipper. '*Offensive*, you mean! Look at this disgraceful muck!'

Gannet, who had naturally taken a strong dislike to the woman, began yapping close to her ankles. The woman's fingers tightened on the handle of her umbrella.

'Come here, Little Wren!' ordered Skipper and obediently Gannet moved behind his heels.

'You happen to have picked upon an active member of the League against Dogs in London Association,' the woman rasped, 'so I should be careful if I were you. I am well acquainted with the law as it relates to dogs.'

'That's interesting, madam, so am I. We apologize for our indiscretion, don't we, Little Wren.'

The woman, who was now seething with anger, unfastened her headscarf to tie it closer round her wispy grey hair, as though for closer protection against this monstrous man and the canine world in general. 'Are you aware that there are over six million dogs in Britain?' she asked Skipper, 'far too many of them in our overcrowded cities, most of them out of control, scaring and sickening citizens like me, causing road accidents, fouling the pavements and the parks, spreading disease.'

Bosun, wearing a vacant grin, was now at Skipper's side. Skipper turned to him. 'Ah, Bosun, old chap, this lady doesn't like dogs, especially' — Skipper cast an eye around for the rest of the pack — 'especially dogs in the park.'

Bosun, taking this as a hint to marshal them, blew his whistle, and, as if from nowhere the other six centred on their masters, furiously tail-wagging. Grenville and Drake put their forefeet on the bench and panted happily at the woman.

'Are these all yours?' the woman hissed at Skipper.

'We are the proud possessors, madam.'

'Then call them away at once! You should be ashamed of yourselves, this park is for people.'

'Come! Come here, all of you!' ordered Skipper. The dogs dutifully fell in behind the two men, and Skipper having indicated that the woman was the focus of attention, stared at her. Nine pairs of eyes were now upon her. Skipper posed like a priest in the pulpit. 'But, madam,' he replied, 'dogs are an important part of nature, some poor townsfolk such as Bosun and me would feel utterly divorced from Mother Nature were it not for the companionship of man's best friend.' Skipper turned on his heel and, proceeded in the direction of Marble Arch, hands clasped behind his back, head held defiantly high, with Bosun and the happy seven in train.

After a hundred yards, he separated a lead from the bundle in his hand and took it towards Gannet. 'Can't trust you, Little Wren,' he told her, clipping it on. 'Don't know your way round here, do you? It's the likes of you that the lady should really have complained of. Yes, *strays*, Little Wren. Did you know,' he asked her, as though the woman's very statistics were contagious, 'that there are 500,000 stray dogs at any given time in Britain, that the Battersea Dogs' Home, to which Bosun and I are about to deliver you, take in 18,000 a year? You knew that, did you? Well, I bet you didn't know that only 5,000 of those Battersea dogs are claimed or bought by visitors. I wonder if anyone'll buy you, eh?' He turned to Bosun and, making the squelching noise in his mouth, drew his forefinger across his throat again. 'I hope, Bosun, that it will not be a question of that for Little Wren.'

Outside the Dogs' Home Bosun held the dogs on the pavement, while Skipper sauntered through the doors. 'Got a damsel in distress, a little lady terrier,' he told the girl at the reception desk. 'Any cabin space on board?'

'There's room,' she replied. 'Will you bring her in . . .'

'It's that daft character from Millbank who thinks he's in the Navy or something,' the girl told the superintendent, when Skipper was out fetching Gannet.

'You mean Skipper? Doubtless his pal Bosun's hovering outside with their pack — or crew, as they call them,' smiled the superintendent, 'and doubtless they've picked up another stray.'

'You're right.'

'Still, you wouldn't find a more responsible couple of dog-owners in London. OK, I'll cope.'

'Did she have that collar and lead when you found her?' the superintendent asked Skipper, when he reappeared with Gannet under his arm.

'No, old boy, they're ours. I'll take them off. She had no means of identification when we found her,' he lied.

Tail between his legs, Gannet was nervous and apprehensive of the daunting, strong-smelling Home. She kept glancing at the entrance, hoping that Mountbatten would follow her.

While the superintendent gave her a closer inspection, Skipper took a look at the expansive notice boards beyond the reception desk, all of them laden with 'wanted' and 'lost' appeals, accompanied by photographs. 'Have you seen our Tommy?' he read, 'very little, very friendly and much beloved by the family, £150 reward.' 'Sad, sad, sad,' muttered Skipper.

'We'll check through those notices later,' promised the superintendent. 'Just sign here, will you?'

'Oh, I don't suppose our Little Wren'd be on your boards, old son. Besides, we'd hate her to be claimed, it being patently clear that her last owners were brutes.'

'Well, as you know, we only keep them for a limited time,' said the superintendent. 'If she's not claimed or bought,' he added in a cold clinical voice that sent a shudder down Skipper's lengthy spine, 'it'll be her bad luck.'

Skipper stopped and held Gannet gently by the ears, looking intently into her eyes. 'Goodbye, Little Wren.' Then, feeling tears on his eyelashes, he stood upright and strode smartly to the entrance door, his Adam's apple working back and forth.

'Bosun,' he said when he rejoined his friend and the other six dogs, 'I've been thinking.'

'What about?'

Skipper stared at Bosun through misty eyes, and wistfully stroked his beard. 'I agree to have Collingwood put down. You've been right all along.'

'Oh, thank you, Skipper, and, by God, Collingwood'll thank you, too — in Heaven.'

CHAPTER FIVE

Gannet was carried to a room that smelled of chloroform. There she was examined all over and treated with an even stronger smelling substance, before being led past a number of blue-and-white painted buildings. She was in the kennels now. She was trotting past rows of pens each furnished with a glass-fibre bed, devoid of cushions, straw or other bedding, but with good underfloor heating. A door was unfastened. She was put in pen number 147 and given a good meal.

The noise was deafening: a continuous barking and whining resounded round the kennels. Since the home stands adjacent to the railways feeding Victoria station the rumbling noise of the trains was almost ceaseless in her ears, too. On one side of her was a dejected greyhound, with seven or eight deep scars on his back and a collapsed pastern; on the other side a liver-and-white spaniel with streaming eyes, whose howling never ceased. Gannet put her nose through the bars, trying to make contact. But the spaniel was too full of self-pity to notice her. Surely Mountbatten would be here somewhere, too? Gannet reached high on to the bars of her pen, peering as far as she could see the other pens, trying to detect his scent through the many unfamiliar scents. The night was far gone before, giving up hope, she retired to curl up on her bleak glass-fibre bed. The noise of the trains and the howling of the dogs abated. But not for long. This place was like a madhouse.

* * *

For the next few weeks during the day the echoing sounds of human footsteps and of clattering bowls and basins, the bustle of kennel-maids mingled with the railway roar. Every morning she heard the Home's van leave to do the rounds of the police stations to collect the London strays, and she heard it return. Sometimes, from sheer boredom she traversed round and round her tiny exercise area until she collapsed panting with giddiness. Then she would start all over again. Other footsteps in the corridors heralded visitors who had paid their 10p in the hope of finding their beloved lost one, or else a pedigree beauty or some engaging half-bred to buy. Gannet, now feeling as lonely and unloved as any Battersea inmate, looked up, as they all did, with beseeching hopeful eyes at every visitor that passed her pen, or who paused, momentarily, to admire her. Gannet, whose puppyhood and first youth at Owlhurst had been all warmth and love and exhilarating sport, now began to harbour a sense of being totally unwanted. But once or twice, she felt stroking fingers pushed through the bars on to her neck and even felt a sense of affection breathing down on her. She wanted desperately to be 'adopted'. And, to her, this meant only one thing — it meant Rose Maxwell.

On the third morning a young man with large horn-rimmed spectacles called out: 'Here's a little beaut' in here, Julie!'

The man's girl-friend crouched at his side, and thrust her fingers into Gannet's pen, caressing her muzzle. 'Sweet, isn't it? . . . but two claws missing on that foot,' she remarked disdainfully. 'We don't want any disfigurements, Bill.' And they, too, passed on, with Gannet's feet clawing frantically at her prison bars, her whine entreating at the couple's backs.

May 13

Gannet's frustration and uneasiness were relieved only by the presence of one particular kennel-girl. She was called Emma, a happy smiling person, whose heart went out to all the dogs, and to Gannet in particular. Although she did not look like Rose — she was a chubby redhead with thick spectacles — her cheerful and affectionate disposition reminded her of Rose. Three weeks after Gannet's arrival at the Home Emma was standing one morning in front of Gannet's pen talking to the superintendent, raising her voice above the pandemonium of dog-howl, the railway and the traffic boom in that unique corner of London.

'I think that one's enchanting,' said Emma, her fingers feeling the busy, loving flick of Gannet's tongue. 'I honestly thought someone would've snapped her up on the first day, and here we are on the twentieth day and no one's even made an enquiry about her.'

The superintendent agreed. 'Lovely little face, isn't it? Conformation's just about faultless, too. Came in looking more than a bit downtrodden; surprising what a few days' Battersea diet does for 'em . . . Just the sort that might pick up prizes in the terrier show rings — in spite of those missing toes.'

Emma bit her lip and frowned. 'All on account of people's ignorance and carelessness. If I was in a position to own a dog, this is the one I'd have I can tell you. This is the one I'll be crying over.' Emma crouched and gave Gannet a kiss where her muzzle protruded from the pen and Gannet wagged her tail and licked the girl's face so furiously that she knocked her glasses off her nose.

The superintendent gazed sadly. 'You wouldn't look that pleased, little dog,' he said, 'if you knew you were here forever.'

What no one knew, except perhaps Gannet herself, was that she was at an early stage of pregnancy.

May 15

Towards the end of the afternoon two days later Emma opened Gannet's door and let the visitor take a close look at her. He was of medium height with an expensive face and sleek black hair. He wore a close-fitting double-breasted pin-stripe and a bow tie while his shoes carried enough polish to pick up every reflection in the kennels.

'She's a little darling, isn't she?' he said, turning to Emma with a well-manicured forefinger on his lips. His city friends, to whom he had confided, advised him — since he had insisted on a Jack Russell — to look down the advertisement columns of the sporting magazines. But Trevor Acland thought better. Ever since boyhood he had harboured faintly romantic ideas about Battersea Dogs' Home.

'She's my favourite,' Emma told him. 'She's obviously got breeding this one, we don't often get terriers with this much quality. It's a wonder she didn't go on her first day here.'

'I'm looking for an anniversary present for my wife; do you think this one'll make a suitable house dog?' Acland's voice verged on the genteel.

Emma adjusted her glasses and scrutinised the man's face for half a second. He didn't look unkind. 'Well, she's got a lovely nature, I can't tell you more than that. Er . . . would she get plenty of exercise? This is a working breed, she'd need a good hour and more a day, preferably off the lead.'

'Good heavens, yes! We live at Hampstead, close to the Heath. Do you happen to know how old she is?'

'Oh, young — at a rough guess, I'd say between two and three.'

Acland pursed his lips and nodded decisively: 'Good, do I pay you, and, if so, how much?'

'You'll be asked to complete a questionnaire. Then you'll be interviewed regarding the lifestyle she'll expect. I should think the cost'll be in the region of thirty to forty pounds. Then there's the vaccination fee, which isn't much.'

'Thank you, I'll definitely take her.'

Gannet, feeling herself supported by the tenderness of Emma's strong forearm, passed the old blue-and-white buildings again and so to the desk where she had arrived a little more than three weeks before. She looked up at the girl. Was she to be taken for a walk at last?

Trevor Acland read the form stating the conditions for purchasing a Battersea dog and signed his name ending it in a fastidious flourish. With much deliberation he chose a collar and lead from the reception shop, fastened the collar, did not like it, selected another, fastened that, held the lead at arm's length, gave a smile and a nod, paid the girl at the desk and, apparently well pleased with his decision, led Gannet to where his Porsche was parked. He opened his brief case, took out the *Daily Telegraph* and smoothed it carefully over the front passenger seat. He then took a fresh yellow duster from the front pocket of the car, wrapped it over Gannet's back, to protect his suit when he picked her up and placed her on the newspaper, raising a cautionary forefinger telling her not to move from there. He decided to call her 'Batty' after Battersea.

Crossing the Thames by Blackfriars Bridge he drove first to Camden Town, where he pulled in by a pet shop and bought some tins of dog meat, plus a cushion and a wicker basket, which the shop had labelled 'suitable for terriers'. He steered the Porsche to Hampstead, eventually turning into Lime Glade, a cul-de-sac flanked by rows of smart mock Tudors, and so down his short garage lane. Looking incongruously exotic in her spotless new yellow collar, Gannet was led up a path to the front door of a house whose stucco even under the mellow light of the sinking May sun, was blindingly white between its black timber beams. Acland's wife was there to meet him in the hall.

'Happy anniversary, darling!' he said, trying coyly to hide

Gannet behind his legs. He faced an ash-blonde woman, trim and *soignée* whose scent reaching Gannet's hypersensitive nostrils was sickly sweet. Everything about the house was immaculate, everything placed just so, highly polished, showing no speck of dust. Gannet's nose caught the odour of furniture polish but the woman's scent was the dominant smell.

A few seconds passed before Mrs Acland noticed Gannet. She looked at a wristwatch studded with tiny diamonds and told her husband he was 'terribly late'.

'I've been busy with your anniversary present, my sweet.'

Mrs Acland looked behind his legs, and put her hand to her mouth aghast, 'Oh, not a *dog!* Oh, Trevor! Who's going to look after it when you're at the office? Goodness me, have you really thought this through?'

'As I said, darling, I wanted Batty as a surprise.'

'It's rather more than that I can tell you. It's quite a shock.'

'I was hoping she would help, well, in a way . . . make up for us not having children.'

'No comment.'

They were in the kitchen now. Trevor Acland, whose face did not disguise his acute disappointment, was opening a tin and spooning it into one of the bowls he had bought at the shop in Camden Town. Gannet sniffed at the food and turned away. She had been very well fed at Battersea. Apart from which, lack of exercise had taken the edge off her appetite. Her only immediate concern was to get out of doors and relieve herself. She crossed to the kitchen door and laid a suggestive paw on it.

'It looks agitated,' said Mrs Acland. 'It'd better not scratch my doors or it'll know all about it.'

Her husband threw her an apologetic look: 'She'll take time to get used to her surroundings . . . Ruth, I'm sorry.'

Another hour passed before either of them thought of letting Gannet out. In a state of great distress and unable to contain herself any longer, she urinated on the kitchen floor. Acland, who was relaxed, in slacks and pullover now, with his newspaper in the sitting-room, heard his wife's scream of 'Oh really!' This is *too* much', and hurried through to see what was the matter.

'Trust you to choose one that isn't even house-trained!' she rounded on him.

'Poor little thing,' Acland sympathised, while tearing off

strips of absorbent paper, 'I expect she's nervous in a strange house.'

'Well, she'll have to learn and learn soon!'

Gannet felt herself scooped off the floor, her nose rubbed in the puddle, and with an 'Ar-r-h, filthy little brute!', thrown out of the back door.

'Oh, I say, have a heart . . .' Acland began.

But his wife would not let him retrieve Gannet. 'If she's to have a place in this house, she must learn the hard way.'

Gannet was confused and hurt, yet she did not cringe as so many of her species would have done. She looked back quizzically at the door. Then she began reconnoitring this new domain. The back garden was about the same size as the front, about twenty yards square with everything neat as a pin. She wandered tentatively following with the closest attention wherever her nose led. She sniffed round the three ornately shaped rose beds whose bushes had been pruned with classic precision and whose grass edges, just clipped for the first time that year, were neat as a starlet's finger-nails.

As this plot seemed to have been allotted to her as her new home, her new territory, she marked it with her scent, raising her hind legs in the handstand attitude that had always so much amused Rose Maxwell. And so she continued to scout and 'occupy' the Acland property, though scarcely approving of it. Here indeed were grass and earth and plants, but they were devoid of the sweet odours of wild pasture, of wild herbs and flowers, of rabbit, rat, fox and badger, giving only the stale urban smells of a cat that had been there the previous evening, garden fertilisers, exhaust fumes and tarmac. Where, she might have wondered, was the great patchwork of fields? Where was the limitless world she had once known, of woodlands, and burrow-combed hedgerows, meadows and streams that surrounded her first lovely home? Surely this was not, after all, to be her permanent territory?

She was in the front garden now. Selecting a bed of dahlias that Acland had planted out the previous weekend, she proceeded to defecate. Acland who was standing at his dining-room windows, about to draw the chintz curtains, spotted her dazzling chestnut-red-and-white figure in the darkening May evening, crouched among his precious annuals. He dashed out in alarm and pulled her on to the lawn, 'No, no, my little Batty,' he cautioned, 'we mustn't do it there, must we?'

His wife, who was witness to the incident, met him in the hall with a mocking laugh. 'I suppose you hadn't thought of that — messes on your precious flower beds! And, if you'll forgive me for quoting my mother again, "there's little that harms a good lawn more than a bitch's pee". There'll be brown patches all over it by the end of the week, my dear, you see.'

'Oh, I don't mind, she's so sweet,' replied Acland with Gannet in his arms.

'*Sweet* indeed! That's not the adjective I'd use. Oh, why, oh, why, couldn't we have discussed this?'

'You'll soon get fond of her, I know you will.'

'I very much doubt it. Now look . . . I think, if we're to prevent your Batty putting us entirely asunder,' she said, 'we must agree that both the hall and the sitting-room are out of bounds, and that she is put out at night.'

Gannet spent that night, the first of several, in the garage. Thoughtlessly, Acland had placed her basket close to the spare petrol can; its fumes were redolent of the car boot on that journey from the canal-side to Clapham. She moved to an oily mat by the opposite wall. Soon after midnight an east wind rose, whistling under the up-and-over door. Curled tight as an indiarubber ball, she shivered until 8.30 the following morning when the door was pulled up with a sudden metallic flourish. The sun flooded in and she was confronted by Acland dressed for the office.

* * *

Life at Lime Glade became intolerable. Trevor Acland proved to be a man of contradictions. He took her to the vet simply because she had been sick from his rich food, and not content with powder and shampoo, he took her a second time in three days because he had found a flea on her. He fed her condition tablets, clipped her claws to their pink and tender quicks, brushed her daily and drooled over her as he might over an adored child. And every time Ruth Acland saw them together, she made the sort of face some wives might have made at finding their husband in the arms of another woman.

On the other hand Acland would, from sheer forgetfulness or ignorance, take Gannet to work, leave her in his car all day with all the windows closed — in what was one of the hottest Mays on record — and then be surprised to find her panting as though she was down to the last breath of oxygen. Not that he was a callous man, or even an unkind one. On the contrary he really loved Gannet. It was just that he was too preoccupied with his own needs and desires, too oblivious of hers. His optimistic remark to the Battersea kennel-girl — 'We live on the edge of Hampstead Heath' — had proved almost meaningless: Gannet had seen little of Hampstead Heath. She disliked her nightly cell, the garage. As for Ruth Acland, she had become increasingly hostile, to the extent that she was now acutely jealous. That was why one morning after ten days of this new life, when Acland opened the garage door and then returned to the house to collect his brief case, Gannet made her bid for freedom and slipped away down the street.

With determination written on her face and on every fibre of her little body Gannet headed along the north London suburban streets leading south. Having failed to discover any new focus to her life, any true home, all her senses were telling her to return to the happy orientation of the place of her upbringing. She hadn't the least conception of how far Owlhurst was, or what obstacles lay in the way; she hadn't even any real memory of the identity of the place; she only knew that in this direction lay the old affection and joy for which she yearned.

It was in a side street in Maida Vale that her journey was interrupted. Heading south, as though on a magnetic bearing and so rigidly that she scarcely looked left or right, she got under the legs of a blind woman led by a guide dog, a German Shepherd. Inadvertently she tripped her up. The German Shepherd seeing her mistress and protector thrown, snarled and bit at Gannet, who barked furiously in return. The woman was soon helped to her feet by a passer-by; but at that moment three schoolboys stopped to watch the commotion. One of the boys, who was eating an apple, threw it with considerable force at Gannet, catching her in the ribs, whereupon Gannet snapped at his ankles. The three boys then danced around her, aiming kicks at her. Within seconds, a tall, horse-faced woman, with a couple of Yorkshire terriers on leads, appeared as from nowhere, brandishing an umbrella at the boys. They scattered like rabbits and, as they ran, a policeman came on the scene. Looping her terriers' leads on her wrist, the horse-faced woman stooped to examine Gannet's collar. Gannet, bewildered by the whole episode, allowed herself to be handled.

'Is it yours?' the policeman asked politely.

'No — no, certainly not, I was just saving it from those little wretches. I'm a dog-owner, as you see, and every inch a dog-lover . . . Here we are, officer, an address on the disc, er — Acland, 3 Lime Glade, Hampstead.' The woman took a spare lead from her raincoat pocket, clipped it on to Gannet's collar, then stood up, squaring herself face-to-face with the policeman. 'Well, now what shall we do?'

'There's a dog warden lives just round the corner from here,' said the constable, 'we'll try him, shall we?'

'Good, lead on, please officer.'

John Anderson, a serious-looking, lean-faced man of forty-five, one of the first dog wardens to be employed by the Borough of Maida Vale, promptly took charge and within half an hour Gannet found herself in his van returning to the home she abhorred. Dog Warden Anderson's knock on the door of 3 Lime Glade and the responding footsteps in the hall sent a shudder through her heart. She knew, all too well, to whom those footsteps belonged.

'Does your dog often go absent? he asked Mrs Acland.

'This is the first time,' she replied, patently annoyed at Gannet's return. 'But it has been a great nuisance.'

'Well, we'll just have to watch it more carefully in future, won't we, madam? It's a long way for a terrier to wander — from here to Maida Vale.'

'Indeed,' said Mrs Acland tensely. 'Will you very kindly put her in the garage and close the door tightly. It's just down there,' she pointed.

'If that's what you want.' Anderson did as he was asked, then returned to the front door. 'Er, just one thing, did you know your dog was pregnant?'

Mrs Acland flinched. 'I did not, I had no idea.'

'My eye tells me she's in her fifth or sixth week. I advise you to take her to your vet to have it confirmed.'

'Oh, my God, this is the end!'

'I'm sorry if I've alarmed you.'

Ruth Acland put on her polite smile. 'It doesn't matter at all . . . Thank you for your advice.'

'Well, I hope she has a lovely litter.'

'Yes. Goodbye, and thank you again.' As she closed the door Ruth Acland's thoughts returned to the subject of her forthcoming visit to her sister, Brenda, in the West Country. This news of Gannet's pregnancy was most tiresome. There was only one thing for it. She must take it to the vet and have the warden's statement endorsed. If it was pregnant the puppies must be destroyed at birth. Better still, she thought to herself, for the bitch to be destroyed. Trevor must be persuaded.

* * *

'Oh, don't worry, darling,' said Acland, with Gannet on his knee. 'She's just a little fat from over-eating. I'll tell you what, I'll put her on a diet and I'll try and put in another five minutes exercise a day.'

Ruth Acland regarded him with a hard, level look. 'She's going to have puppies. I've taken her to the vet, he's confirmed it.'

'Well, I think that's wonderful news, frankly I'm delighted,' he beamed, still gazing down at Gannet. 'I'll rear them myself and we'll sell them. What fun we'll have.'

'Oh, yes, brilliant idea,' replied his wife with all the sarcasm she could muster. 'As I told you — though I don't think it ever sunk in — my parents had a bitch that had puppies when I was a child, and those puppies made me sick, literally sick. They had to be fed four times, if not five, a day . . . And who's going to do that with this lot, may I ask? Not me, I assure you. Perhaps you're going to take a couple of months off from work?'

'I think you'll come round to Batty's puppies, darling, I really do.'

'No comment.'

'Well, what do you suggest?'

She inclined her head at him and shook it slowly. 'Well, I hate to be this blunt, but, let's face it, your Batty's come between us. I don't believe I can take this much longer. I honestly think we'll have to get rid of her — have her put down or give her away.'

At that, Acland's expression changed to one of such pain that his wife felt sorry for him for the first time since Gannet's arrival. She put her hands on his arms. Gannet winced. 'Oh, don't look so miserable — it's all been a great misunderstanding, hasn't it?' She pushed Gannet on to the floor and kissed him lightly on the forehead.

'And you're driving down to Brenda tomorrow — for two whole nights,' said Acland. 'I hate to think of you hating Batty and her puppies all the way there and back.'

Mrs Acland stood up, arms akimbo. 'Now, look, Trevor, I want a promise out of you before I leave. We either have Batty put to sleep nice and painlessly or we arrange to pass her on to new owners within a week. Which is it to be?'

Acland bit his lower lip, gathered Gannet on to his knees again and, shaking his head, started stroking her thoughtfully. 'I couldn't,' he said at last, 'I just couldn't.'

'Well, let me tell you this — it may well be a question of you choosing between me and her.'

In her garage bed that night Gannet dreamed of Elysian fields and of a kennel-girl she had loved. But in fits and starts she kept waking. The noise of the London traffic just beyond kept reminding her that she was still in this hell: she had to escape again.

May 27

Ruth Acland woke again, too. She had not slept well. Now the dim light of dawn filtered through the curtains. She switched her bedside torch on to the clock. Ten minutes past five. She glanced across at her husband's form. He slept heavily in the morning, nearly always slept late and was usually deaf to the alarm. She got up slowly and carefully groped for her clothes, took them to the bathroom, dressed very hurriedly, and tiptoed downstairs. She gave herself some coffee and cornflakes and laid a place for him. Then she wrote a note, which she propped against his breakfast cup: 'Darling, I hope I didn't wake you. Disaster! When I opened the garage door, Batty dashed out under my feet. Cat by the gate. Batty made a dash for it. Ran to the gate and saw then careering down the Glade full tilt. Called her and called her. But completely vanished. Very early so didn't like to bother you. 'Spect she's back by the time you see this. Everything in fridge for you. See you day after tomorrow. Love R.'

Ruth Acland took her suitcase to the garage, put it in the car boot and gave Gannet a cold lingering glance. Gannet looked back in trepidation. Then Mrs Acland snatched her off her basket, thrust her on to the rear seat and closed the door. No sooner did Gannet hear the click of the door than she was filled with a terrible premonition.

There was, however, a witness to Mrs Acland's departure

that morning. David Young, a friend of the Aclands and resident of 4 Lime Glade, happened to be standing at his bedroom window sipping his early morning tea at that time. Gannet, jumping up against the car's rear window, looking back, was clearly visible. Young, aware that Ruth was on her way to visit her sister, wondered casually why she was taking Batty with her.

For the whole of the first three hours of the journey — through London and on the M4 — Mrs Acland rationalized her intention. Trevor was quite clearly and irrevocably besotted with this terrier, which she, Ruth, detested. The dog threatened the cohesion, the future, the very continuation of their marriage. If this dog, this ridiculous wedding anniversary present, stayed, there would be a separation, divorce proceedings might even have to begin.

All that was unthinkable. It was not right or fair that a mere dog should be allowed to come between her and Trevor like this. Batty must be sacrificed on the altar of their marriage. It would not be an expensive sacrifice, nor necessarily even a cruel one. But it had to be done for both their sakes, it was imperative. It would be easy — she would simply 'lose' Batty. Trevor would never know. He would read the note on the kitchen table, he would go in search of the dog, perhaps for ten minutes, then shrug and drive to the office expecting Batty to have returned by the evening. Disappointed, he would telephone the police and the nearest animal shelter. He would certainly call the Battersea Home. He would mourn Batty briefly. But he would have learned his lesson, he would never buy another dog.

The rain turned from drizzle to downpour. Ruth Acland switched her windscreen wiper from slow to fast. In the early morning light on the wet shining road the wiper was like a tragic song's fateful refrain: 'It must be done, it must be done, the dog must go, the dog must go.'

At Bristol she swung south-west on to the M5. Five miles beyond the Taunton turning she pulled on to the hard shoulder, got out into the driving rain, plucked Gannet from the rear seat, placed her on the grass, got back behind the wheel and continued her journey with a deep sigh of relief.

The business was done and that was that. She looked in her driving mirror with just a twinge of conscience and one last fleeting look at the tan-and-white terrier shivering in the downpour.

Gannet gazed through the slanting rain at Mrs Acland's receding tail-light. Although her instinct told her she'd been deserted in a faraway place, she felt a sudden lightness of mood at being relieved of that woman's oppressive company. The motorway leviathans were splashing her. The crazy, human rush, the race to be first, the traffic boom, were petrifying. She retreated up the bank and crouched shuddering against the remorseless rain. Then she shook herself and turned her muzzle eastwards.

* * *

The only background noise at Owlhurst that morning was the occasional surge of music from thirty-three-and-a-half couple of foxhounds, interjected every half-hour or so by the drone of an aircraft flying in to or from Gatwick airport. At 8.30, fifteen minutes after the visit from the newsagent's man, a girl's excited shout was heard in the huntsman's office.

'I'm certain it's her, Ted. I'm certain it's her!' cried Rose with the tabloid spread out on the office table. Her eyes were fixed on a photograph entitled *May Happiness by the Chelsea Embankment.* It showed a tall, smiling, bearded man with a nautical cap hanging over one ear, reclining on a public bench with a Jack Russell terrier on his chest and another terrier between his knees, and pigeons fighting for crusts on the ground just below him.

'What is it, then?' said Jennings.

'Look at this snapshot . . . the dog on the man's chest, the markings on the head, the patch on the side, the profile. I think I can even see where the toes are missing. I'm going to get a magnifying glass. Anyhow, it's Gannet, I swear it!'

Ted Jennings looked very dubious. 'How could she've been in London? Now you tell me that.'

'I can't imagine. All I know is that there's no other terrier in the world that could match up as well.'

'Do you just? Well, you'll have to find the gent in the picture first. You'd sooner find a needle in haystack,' Jennings laughed.

'You just wait, Ted. Here's the name of the photographer — Sarah Bailey. I'm going to ring the newspaper offices and get in touch with her. Maybe she's got the man's name to send a print to or something.'

'And maybe she ain't.'

By midday Rose had contacted the newspaper's art department and secured Sarah Bailey's home number. By 6 o'clock she had spoken to Sarah Bailey, who had given her the address of the bearded man in the picture. He was called Jack Poynter and lived at a Millbank address. Sarah Bailey was 'thrilled to bits' with the picture: 'I'd almost given up hope of it being used. It was taken three weeks ago. I'm over the moon.' By ten minutes past six Rose had been informed by directory enquiries that the number she required was ex-directory. At 7 o'clock she was telling Luke of her progress and he was agreeing to accompany her to the Millbank address the following afternoon. By this time Luke felt so deeply attached to her that he could, as he admitted, refuse her nothing.

CHAPTER SIX

Squatting on the motorway embankment, looking down on the furious traffic, awe-inspired, mesmerized by it, Gannet had never seemed so small, never so vulnerable. Although she was not to know that she was separated by a huge distance from the place she loved, she was conscious of being totally lost, totally deserted. Nor had she any doubt that she had been deliberately abandoned. The experiences of the past five weeks had taught her to rely very little on the faithfulness or compassion of mankind. Yet she knew she could not live without man. Every square meal, with which she had ever been blessed, had come from 'him'. She must therefore use first her nose and second her eyes and legs to find a new protector. She had to put distance between herself and the splashing road. Since man had never allowed her to become acclimatized to the extremes of weather, but had always provided a roof against the elements, she must find a roof now, a shelter against this unremitting downpour that struck through her thin coat to the pores of her skin. Shaking herself, she was alert again.

Without hesitation or doubt, her senses pointed her due east, and having climbed the motorway bank, that was the way she began to trot. By midday the rain had ceased, soon her smart red-and-white coat was dry and she revelled in all those sights and sounds and odours of which she had been deprived since the Owlhurst days. The earth felt good under her feet, the grass smelt sweet, the trees were in small young leaf, and Somerset was vibrant with birdsong. The sense of freedom was marvellous. Longing to rid herself of the stink of the Hampstead house, to render herself a true child of Nature she rolled her back luxuriously in several patches of dung. Now, nostrils to the ground, this way and that she indulged in the traces of rabbit. But as she was yet neither hungry, nor inclined to hunt, but only intent upon returning to places and people of her origins, she continued more or less unwaveringly on her instinctive compass bearing.

After six hours trek, which brought her within a few miles of Curry Rivel, she wandered into an old barn full of hay bales, on the edge of a farm complex. At her approach two cats ran off, their tails standing up like bottle brushes. She was very weary. In a corner she found a pile of loose hay. She curled up in the middle of it and slept soundly until long after daybreak.

She awoke very suddenly, alarms flooding on to her senses. She was threatened and the threat was very close to her.

* * *

Rose turned to Luke with a happy sigh and a smile of relief at finding the name 'Mr R. Poynter' by the bell that rang the basement flat of the Millbank house.

Below it they read 'Mr B. Birkin.'

'There!' she said, pressing the knob, 'so we've tracked him down.'

They rang four times. There was no reply.

'Let's go and knock,' suggested Luke.

The curtains of the basement window were drawn tight. They climbed to the main entrance and rang the bell to the first-floor flat. A jovial red-faced woman, opened the door.

'Hello, love, what can I do for you?'

'So sorry to bother you. We're looking for Mr Poynter.'

'Oh, 'Skipper', and his friend, Mr Birkin — ''Bosun'', they call him. Quite a pair they are. I'm Mrs Hitchings, a friend of theirs like.'

'We tried to telephone,' explained Luke, 'but they're ex-directory.'

'That's right, very private people are Skipper and Bosun, keep themselves to themselves, don't like to be bothered, you understand? Like to go their own way, but good pals of mine they are.'

'Do you happen to know where they are?'

'Well, Skipper did say they were going to see his old mother in Lincolnshire. She's nearly ninety, I believe; wonderful, isn't it?'

'Does Mr Poynter still keep dogs?' asked Luke.

The woman gave a high-pitched chortle. 'Lor' bless my soul, do Skipper and Bosun still keep dogs? Are you trying to pull my leg or something? I should say they do. There must be half a dozen of them at least. Every sort and description, big and little, and all the colours of the rainbow, I should say. They make a fair old noise sometimes, too . . . But Skipper and

Bosun are a nice couple of gents, see, so I don't mind really. They're quite famous for their pooches round these parts. If there's dogs around, you don't get burglars, least you're not so likely to -'

'Mr Poynter was photographed earlier this month with a couple of tan-and-white terriers,' Rose interrupted her. 'We've a feeling one of them's a stray that was once mine. She's called Gannet. She is — was — a marvellous companion and I miss her terribly. If you can help . . .'

The woman gave her forefinger a wipe on her dress and put it to her lips reflectively. 'Is that right? Well they've got one like that — it's the one they call Mountbatten, I think. They're all named after famous admirals. They are a funny couple,' she giggled. 'Yes, and come to think of it there was a stranger for a day, two or three weeks back, a female it was — all their other lot are males. More red-and-white than tan-and-white, lovely little thing, if I remember rightly, though it did look a bit cut up. Don't know that they've still got it, though. Them dogs come and go like I don't know what. Well, they're back day after tomorrow so you can call again.'

Rose and Luke's eyes met happily.

'Oh, thank you, Mrs Hitchings!' said Rose. 'I'll come back then.'

'Call about lunchtime, love. They're out exercising "the crew", as they call them, most other times. Goodbye, then.'

When Mrs Hitchings closed the door Rose put a hand on Luke's shoulder and kissed him lightly on the cheek. 'Thank you for coming, Luke. Now I *know* we're going to find her.'

'We're nearly there,' said Luke, returning the kiss, radiant as a child at Christmas. 'Very nearly home and dry.'

'The day after tomorrow,' Rose repeated.

* * *

Lifting her nose from the crook of her hock in her nest of hay, chestnut ears pricked, white hackles rising, Gannet faced a rough-coated brindle dog with heavily loaded shoulders, very fierce-looking and one of the largest she had ever seen, as tall as an Irish wolfhound, but much thicker set at every point. Two farm cats raced from the barn, their coats and tails all a-bristle.

She strutted to one side of him, snarling as she moved.

With a long, low growl he circled in towards her, heavy feet pressing deep into the hay, yellow eyes blazing. She stepped nimbly away, keeping her distance like a flyweight facing a heavyweight. Showing yellow teeth, two of them broken, with a long low growl the brindled giant tried to manoeuvre her towards the barn wall. But Gannet stood her ground. This was where she'd slept; so far as she was concerned at this moment this was her territory. He barked venomously close to her face; she snapped at his muzzle, bit him on the lip, drawing blood. He jumped back with an expression of surprise, like Goliath before David. Barking with all her might, Gannet held him at bay. Then she heard a human voice.

''Ere, Shiner, y'clot, what y'got in there, eh, lad?'

Not taking her eyes off her adversary Gannet was aware of the presence of two men at the open side of the barn. Their very aura evoked memories of human evil, of Trench, of Mrs Slater, of Mrs Acland. When Gannet was reminded of unkind people it was their hands and feet that were uppermost in her senses, hands that slapped and cuffed and buffeted, feet that kicked. It was not fear of the brindled giant dog that made her shiver now, it was phantom hands and feet that flooded her emotions when she heard the mean tone of voice echoing through the barn. One of the men held a second dog, a Dobermann, on a lead.

'There's a bit of sport to be 'ad 'ere, Joe,' the first voice sounded again. 'Little scavenging terrier should give a spot of fun to a couple of good country lads like us. Let's see 'em rip it up, eh?'

'Yeah, yeah, perishin' little stray, let's get 'em in at it!' The second man unclipped the Dobermann's leash. 'Get in there, Shot!' he ordered. 'Seek, seek. Tear it up, lad!'

Gannet now faced the two of them, the brindled one thick as a St Bernard, and on the other side, the crimson-jowled Dobermann with an ear-splitting bark. Cornered, she growled back, strutting this way and that, parrying their advances. Notwithstanding her terror she took in the situation in a flash. These dogs were mostly bark, little bite. They had the sort of impotent viciousness that sprang from a life of rough handling, of ill-treatment. But the men were infinitely more dangerous. She must make a dash for it. But which way?

''Ere, Bill, don't let it get out! You and me circle round the edge, right?'

'OK, I'm goin' to grab that pitchfork.'

Gannet's eyes must be on the two men as well as the two dogs. The one called Bill advanced on her with a pitchfork, swaying it this way and that, ready to catch her on any line of retreat. His sidekick swung a leash in full circles towards her, its metal clip whipping menacingly through the hay at each downward curve of his swing. The two dogs stood between them closely facing Gannet, continuously snarling. She seemed to be trapped. She was poised to take advantage of the best means of escape. She would avoid the men, risk the dogs.

'Right, we've got it now, Joe. Little Jack Russell, ain't it? 'Ave at it Shiner! Tear it up, Shot.'

A split second before any of them reacted Gannet flew fast as an arrow between the two dogs. She jinked to the left of a pile of hay bales, under a tractor and down the side of the barn. The pitchfork, thrown like a javelin, clattered against the wall, its handle falling sharply on her back. With a quick yelp of pain she twisted round the entrance of the barn.

'Go on, Shiner!'

'Get after it, Shot!'

The two dogs who had not dared to move until those commands were given, bounded after her, but within thirty seconds, Gannet left them lumbering far behind.

On she raced — she who was once fêted by the Westdown hunt as a great terrier, but was now branded as a 'scavenger' and 'a dirty stray' — east, east, east.

Four hours later she was down to a very slow trot. She felt much more tired than on yesterday's journey. And she was ravenously hungry. She yearned as never before for the bowlfuls of rich food that man had put down for her so regularly, and at which she had so often turned up her nose. She had sniffed round three or four farmyards in vain. Twice this morning, too, she had been within inches of the scuts of young rabbits and had slavered at the thought of them. She did not feel famished simply for herself, but also for the new life she felt within her. The will to live, to nourish her body, was no longer for herself alone, but for something that was growing inside her, something she was creating. Slowly, but strongly, she was developing a maternal sense and with it a reduction in her old athletic self. But just when she needed food most she was least able to hunt and kill it.

She spent her second night of abandonment in the bole of

a dead oak tree, through which the wind whistled with all the urgency of an express train's warning.

May 29

The next day found her pointing along the grass verge of a minor road — east, east, and ever east, like an explorer on a fixed bearing. The road came to a sharp bend. East was straight on. She started to cross the road to make for a gap in the opposite hedgerow and the cornfield beyond it. Rose had taught her in puppyhood to beware of the tarmac highways. She broke into a quick trot.

A deafening roar of motorbikes, sudden as the first thunderclap that interrupts the lull before a storm, broke the silence of the countryside. Gannet panicked. The leading bike went into a screaming skid, catching her with the silvery hub of its rear wheel on the thigh. Letting out an abrupt squeal of agony, she rolled over three times like a little barrel, then got up, lame, dazed, walking on three legs, three or four paces in short steps, head low, tail-stump pressed between her buttocks, recoiling at the shock. The motorbikes were both pulled up now, humming in neutral.

'Bliddy little tyke, might have killed me!' shouted the rider.

'Is she 'urt bad?' asked his mate, wheeling his bike up alongside and staring superciliously at Gannet. Both were dressed from head to foot in silver-studded black leather. They cut out their engines.

'I dunno 'bout that,' answered the rider who had bumped Gannet, removing his helmet. 'All I know is people ought to be locked up what let their tykes wander round loose.'

Gannet sat in a hunched position watching them, too hurt and dazed to make any deliberate move.

'Tell you something,' said his mate, 'tykes like that fetch money, 'n' you and me's short.'

'That's right. Nice looking little terrier. I got a badger-baitin' friend could use this one.'

'You mean Mike?'

'Yeah, he can't do with enough of 'em. It ain't got no collar, so it don't belong to anyone.'

'It's a Jack Russell. My Uncle Bert had a Jack Russell. It

looks a bit tucked up right now, but with a bit of . . . Yeah, that's it, why don't we sell it? Could get forty quid.'

They both laughed loudly. Gannet, physically numb, still didn't move, but simply watched them. The second rider leaned down and rubbed his fingers at her. 'C'mon, little tyke!' Gannet kept her distance. The rider opened one of his panniers, took out a paper bag, extracted a sausage roll, broke off an end of it, and leaned low towards her again. 'C'mon then, nice grub!' Gannet, walking painfully and weakly on three legs, approached the proffered morsel. A hint of the rich meat and pastry wafted towards her and her nostrils quivered. Being forty-eight hours without food and six weeks pregnant, the lure was overwhelming. She slavered. The riders saw the saliva drip from her jowl. But Gannet was determined not to be in the grip of bad people again. She aimed to grab the food, then retreat sharply. In her present condition, however, weak, tired, dazed and injured, she wasn't quick enough. The moment her teeth were on the sausage, the rider's hand shot out and grasped her by the neck. She wriggled and fought with every ounce of such strength as she had. But it was no good. In a trice the youth had stuffed her into his other pannier and strapped it tight. The space was so tight there was hardly room to move, let alone to struggle.

Gannet yapped in that plastic cage as she had never yapped before. She yapped with full throat at all mankind. The noise, though stifled and muffled, irritated her captor. 'Aw, shaddap! Shut yer dirty little trap!' he shouted, picking up his helmet by the chinstrap and swinging it full force against the pannier. Gannet's howl of outrage was reduced to a whimper.

''Ere, careful, Art, that could be forty quid's worth we got in there!'

The first rider put on his helmet, swung a leg over the saddle, kicked the starter, revved up and turned to his mate. 'Have a yob about it at the 'Are and 'Ounds shall we then?'

'OK,' shouted the second youth, holding up a thumb of assent, ''Are and 'Ounds and your turn to pay, mate!'

* * *

The telephone rang at 3 Lime Glade. Ruth Acland watched and listened as her husband answered.

'Yes, that's right . . . yes . . . Good heavens, in Somerset? How on earth did it get there? You may be right . . . Yes, send it, please, if you would, I'll return the cost of postage the moment it arrives. That's very kind, thank you for your trouble.' He replaced the receiver slowly, continuing to look at it, brow furrowed.

'Who was it, Trevor?'

Still wearing his puzzled expression, Acland faced his wife. 'Would you believe it,' he said, 'Batty's collar's been found in Somerset of all places. These people had a puncture on the M5, pulled into the hard shoulder and found Batty's collar. They're sending it back.'

Reddening, Ruth passed her tongue nervously between her scarlet lips. 'How extraordinary! I suppose someone must have picked her up when she'd finished chasing the cat out here, took her down to the West Country, and jettisoned the collar, so she couldn't be identified.' Ruth cursed herself for not thinking of burying the give-away article, or discarding it somewhere else.

Her husband regarded her quizzically. 'You were on the M5. Uncanny to think you probably passed a few yards from the collar on your way back from Brenda.'

'Oh, darling, you do have such funny trains of thought!'

He noticed how agitated her fingers were as she patted her well-groomed hair. 'Do I?' he said 'Seems quite logical to me.'

As though to dismiss the subject she took him by the shoulders with a laugh and a kiss. 'You funny old thing! Well, that's the last we'll hear of Batty. We can only hope she had a merciful end.'

'What do you mean by that? She's not dead.'

Busy as Ruth was trying to look composed, she knew that she was not thinking properly. 'I mean . . . I mean dogs don't last long in the hands of people who steal them.'

'My intuition tells me she's very much alive.'

Ruth gave another nervously contrived laugh. 'Oh, you and your intuition!'

'I loved that little dog. I'm beginning to feel guilty I didn't give her a better time here.'

Ruth shook her head from side to side, impatiently. 'Oh, forget the little brat.'

'Are you sure she chased a cat that morning?'

'I'm not a liar,' said Ruth walking out of the room and closing the door.

Her words 'dogs don't last long in the hands of people who steal them', resounded again and again in Acland's mind as he was left by himself in the silence of the sitting-room.

* * *

The weaving high-speed passage in the motorbike pannier was more nightmarish for Gannet than her journey in the Bryants' car boot. Then she had been so preoccupied with passive fighting — fighting for air, fighting against thirst, fighting against the sickness brought on by the petrol can, fighting to stay alive — that she was spared the other terror. But, despite her present tribulations, she had all her wits about her now, and the close, coal-black claustrophobic imprisonment in this plastic case, accentuated by the contrast of her recent liberty and compounded by the speed and swerving of the bikes, brought a panic on her. For several minutes while the engines roared she scratched, so far as the minute space would allow, at the top of her black cage and whined. Then, feeling sick, she gave up the effort and was reduced to cringing numbness. Soon the bikes came to a standstill, their engines ceased and they were leaned over to rest.

The sound of the youths' hobnails receded along the car park gravel. Gannet wriggled her nose against the pannier's flaps and managed to push her way between the straps, exposing an eye to the daylight, thus receiving a narrow view of the car park. She tried to get a paw up, but failed. Ten minutes later a car pulled up next to the bikes. Two middle-aged women stepped out. One of them, an expansive figure, stood close to her with a pained air about her puffy face.

'Oh, look, Mavis, look at this poor little thing!' A podgy finger was lowered to Gannet's muzzle. Gannet licked it. It might be friendly. She felt it stroking her.

'Well, I never,' said the other one. 'It's not fair, is it? Whoever it belongs to ought to be ashamed of themselves, keeping a pet in a place it can hardly move itself. I'd give 'em a piece of my mind.'

The fat one paused. 'I'd give them more than that. I think it's really shocking. I'm going to let it out.' The fat fingers went to the straps and buckles.

'No, Dot, I wouldn't, honestly I wouldn't. You interfere with other people's business nowadays you get yourself beaten up, you only have to read the papers . . . especially the likes as ride speed bikes. Let's report it to the police, dear, that's best.'

The well-covered woman, who was returning Gannet's pleading eye with a sentimental one, did not agree. 'Oh, don't be daft, the man'd be back to the bike and gone by the time we got the police. You might as well write a letter to the RSPCA for all the good that'd do. I'm not standing by seeing a dog treated like this. I'll just open the flap and see what the poor little thing *wants* to do. It might stay there for all we know.'

Her friend kept looking apprehensively over her shoulder at the pub door. 'Well, if you're going to do it, for Pete's sake hurry, Dot, the owner's not going to thank you for it.'

Gannet felt the quick fumble of the fat fingers on the straps again.

'Oh, quick, Dot, quick, there are two young blokes coming out of the pub all in motorbike gear!'

No sooner were both buckles unfastened than Gannet was out, sharp as a greyhound from a stadium trap, scuttling across the car park gravel on three legs.

'There, look at that, Mavis, hopping lame, did you see, and a big cut on its leg, downright shame!'

'Oh, poor thing — terrified!'

There were ominous crunches on the gravel behind.

''Ere, what are you at then?' came the first voice. 'Did you let our dog out?'

'Oh, it's yours, is it?'

''Course it's perishin' well ours, seein' it's in our pan-yer.'

'Oh, poor thing, it was near to choking in there . . . must have been like a strait-jacket.'

'You let it out, you did!'

'We never, it let itself out.'

'I saw you, you interferin' old cow!'

'You never saw, 'cos we didn't; it let itself out. It was in such a state, it . . . it tore itself free. We saw it!'

The youths stood tall and close and menacing above the women. The voice took on a sarcastic quality now.

'Oh? And the little tyke undid the straps, I suppose?'

'Well, we didn't do it. Anyway you ought to be that ashamed of yourselves keeping a . . .'

The youths did not hear the end of the woman's homily. They had crossed to the road and were searching left and right. But there was no sign of Gannet.

'C'mon, Dot, let's drive off, I don't feel like a drink now.'

Dot had not hesitated. She was already behind the wheel with the engines running and Mavis found herself climbing into the passenger seat as the car was moving off.

'Do you think it'll fend for itself, Dot, or do you think those nasty boys'll find it?'

'Get run over, likely as not. I did read somewhere that dogs cause half a million road accidents a year.'

'Ninety-nine times out of a hundred it's the owner's fault.'

'Well, I hope we did the poor darling a good turn.'

'I hope so, too.'

The motorcycle ride having carried her south-east, Gannet was now heading resolutely east-north-east, still on three legs and sore where her thigh was cut and swollen. A little after dark she came to a larch copse. She took the broad moonlit ride that cut through the middle of it. She was half way along it when a roe deer, obviously frenzied with fear, shot from one side to the other, its white rump showing bright under the moon. Right behind it came half a dozen dogs, and, moments after that, Gannet felt the dazzling beam of torchlight on her eyes.

'Hey, Ted, little terrier all by itself on three legs!' the voice behind the torch shouted. But, whoever Ted was, being too intent on the venison and the money it would bring, did not hear, but ran on across the ride after the dogs. Now a third poacher carrying a gun as well as a torch, crossed the ride. Gannet shrank away into the cover of the larches. Half a minute later she heard the dogs baying in a terrible chorus, then the sound of both barrels of a shotgun rang out through the night.

She hurried on, jumped the ditch that bounded the larch plantation and traversed the headlands of four fields of young corn before arriving at a beech wood. There she found a hedgehog whose smell reminded her of her acute hunger. Balancing on two legs, she tried to unroll its ball. She bit at it; its prickles penetrated her gums and tongue. In her frustration she barked furiously at it. Her noise alarmed the roosting birds. Pigeons clattered from the branches above her, a pheasant rocketed away with an angry call and whirring wings. Penetrating the wood she found some straw. From old Owlhurst experience, this vaguely reminded her of pheasants and all the hazards connected with game preservation, the sort of hazards that had lost her two toes in a trap. But she was so weary and weak from hunger and pain and the effort of travelling several miles on three legs that she lay thankfully on the straw and fell to licking her wound.

Soon black clouds hid the moon, and a heavy rain began. She curled herself, tight as that reluctant hedgehog, against the torrent and shivered till dawn. The silence was broken by the sounds, among other avian voices, of the cheeping of waking pheasant chicks. She had slept close to a rearing pen. When she got up and stretched, she found herself stiffer than ever in her injured leg, and her walk was reduced to a hobble.

May 30

Rose drove back to London by herself that morning, Luke being tied to his surgery.

Skipper, who had been told of her visit two days before, opened the door of the basement bed-sitting-room bidding her: 'Welcome aboard, ma'am, ship's company resting . . . This is my friend, Bosun.' The smell of dogs was overwhelming. Quick as a flash Rose's eye, yearning for Gannet, traversed their reposing bodies, hoping against hope to spot the little red-and-white figure curled up behind one of them. Giving a sigh of disappointment she produced the press photograph of Skipper, Mountbatten and Gannet, together with a coloured one of Gannet of her own.

'You see? Matches up exactly.'

'Ay, my dear,' said Skipper, eyeing Rose's portrait of Gannet, 'that's our Little Wren, all right.' He took the label from the Alexander Kent paperback. 'She had this tied to her collar — and guess what her collar was? Piece of orange-coloured twine.'

'Doggie Bryant, 63 Plane Tree Road, Clapham,' Rose read. 'Did you give her back to them, then?'

'Shiver my timbers, no! People who keep a dog in that condition didn't deserve to have dogs. We took her into Battersea, my dear.'

Rose's face lit up like the dawn of a spring day. 'Oh, just across the river — I'll go and claim her.'

'Well, it *was* over a month ago. Do you recall the date, Bosun?'

Bosun was prompt on dates: 'April 22nd.'

'Ah, yes,' replied Skipper. 'Well, I'm rather afraid she'll have been snapped up by now, my dear.'

As Skipper closed the door behind Rose, Bosun glanced up at him. 'That reminds me, Skipper, I've got a lot to thank that Little Wren for.'

'What in particular?' asked Skipper.

'Well, it was only our discussing her future and putting her in Battersea that led you to agree to having poor old Collingwood put down.'

Skipper looked at his friend silently for a few moments. 'You promised never to mention Collingwood's name again,' he said at last. 'God rest his poor old red setter soul.'

* * *

Hopes still running high, Rose crossed Battersea Bridge, found a parking space and was in the Home within minutes. Having received her training at an affiliated kennel-maid training school, Rose had visited the Battersea home on several occasions and knew just how to start her enquiry. In no time at all it led to Emma, the girl who had looked after Gannet, a girl after Rose's heart.

'Oh, yes, *full* of character!' said Emma, scrutinising Rose's photograph. 'And the most affectionate and attractive terrier I've ever had in my care. I bored them stiff telling everyone here that, if I could have owned a dog, which I can't, that's the one I'd have had.'

'What was he like?' asked Rose. 'I mean the man who bought her.'

'Oh, rather a smooth-tongued, forty-ish, smartly dressed City type. They'll give you his details at the reception . . . Best of luck, then!'

'May 15 . . . Trevor Acland, 3 Lime Glade, Hampstead,' the book told her. She borrowed a directory and rang his house. No reply. She glanced at her watch. 5.40. A 'City' man, was he? Well, he'd probably be in by the time she got there.

No sooner was she back in her car then she was pin-pointing the smart north London residential avenue on her street plan; and, driving in its direction, she came to thinking about Luke; it was really Gannet who had brought her and Luke together. The trials of the last few weeks would have been so much harder without his support. The days of Leonard

Trench seemed like a distant, ugly nightmare and she was glad that Martin Eliot was diverted by Camilla Dewar. A year ago she would not have dreamed that Luke could be the man in her life. Now it was as though there could never really have been anyone else. 'And this evening,' she thought, 'I am on the way to see my Gannet again . . . It seems unbelievable. But how on earth am I going to persuade this Mr Acland to give her up? I can't *make* him do it; after all, Gannet's his now. Maybe I can persuade him into taking one of the new Owlhurst puppies in lieu. I wonder what Gannet's reaction will be when she sees me?' Rose drove through the City at a most determined pace. Being in love she looked radiant.

Hope welling in her like a tidal wave Rose pressed hard on the bell of 3 Lime Glade.

Ruth Acland opened the door: 'Good evening, what can I do for you?'

'I'm very sorry to bother you. I tried to phone. I lost my Jack Russell terrier six weeks ago, and . . .'

'Oh, dear, how careless of you!' Ruth interrupted her.

'. . . and I've just come from Battersea Dogs' Home and they told me that Mr Acland -'

Ruth Acland, looking very tense, interrupted again: 'Really, how interesting. Your name is . . .?'

'Maxwell, Rose Maxwell.'

'I see . . . well, my husband has just got home. It's not a very convenient time, but perhaps you'd like to speak to him.'

Rose was ushered into the hot and sophisticated sitting-room, pervaded by the sickly scent that Mrs Acland wore.

Her husband was hidden behind his newspaper.

'This is Miss Maxwell — she seems to think that Batty was hers. She's just come from the Dogs' Home.'

'Good evening.' Acland got up, holding out a hand and smiling pleasantly.

'*Was?*' said Rose.

Acland shook his head sadly. 'I'm afraid she went missing three days ago.'

Rose gave an inaudible sigh of disappointment, a groan.

'I'm so sorry,' Acland continued, 'but first let's be certain that she was yours, shall we?'

Rose had already taken the photograph from her handbag.

Acland replaced his reading glasses and examined it closely. 'Yes . . . amazing . . . yes, it must be.'

'She was missing two toes on a forefoot,' Rose added.

Acland glanced up quickly. 'Was she indeed? Well that confirms it. Look, I hate to tell you this, but we think she was stolen. I had a telephone call from Somerset. Her collar — that's the collar I bought for her — was picked up on the side of the M5 near Taunton. It's in the post to us now. Of course, I've reported the loss all over the place, including the animal shelters in the Taunton area.'

Ruth turned her head away from them.

Rose bit her lip, choking back the tears she felt welling and stinging behind her eyelids.

'What a myth it is about dogs' faithfulness,' said Ruth. 'Batty — or Gannet as you call her — ran after a cat here three days ago just as I was leaving to stay with my sister in Devon and we never saw her again after that. We gave her a wonderful life and yet she deserted us.'

'Or, rather, was stolen,' her husband corrected her.

'It was quite unnecessary of her to get herself stolen,' put in Mrs Acland.

'I must disagree with you about her character,' retorted Rose, who noticed how hard the woman's face had remained. 'Gannet was the most faithful, the most brave, the most loving little dog I've ever known.'

'That,' replied Ruth, 'is very difficult to believe.'

Her husband turned to Rose. 'I absolutely agree with Miss Maxwell; Batty has a totally faithful character and I'm sure she's alive somewhere — somewhere. Will you leave us your telephone number?'

Rose tore a page from a pocket notebook and jotted down her address and number.

Ruth twisted her fingers together, looked grimly at her husband for a moment, then, moving towards the sitting-room door, she faced Rose again: 'Well, we'll certainly let you know if there's any news of Batty. But, if I were you, I wouldn't hold out much hope.' She opened the door with a patent gesture of farewell. 'Goodbye.'

'Goodbye,' said Rose. 'And thank you.'

She drove straight home, her mind full of confusion. There was something fishy about the Aclands. They didn't seem to trust one another. Mrs Acland appeared to be covering up in some way. Acland's affection for Gannet was obviously quite as strong as his wife's dislike of her. Yet he didn't seem at all like a 'doggy' man. 'I'm sure she's alive,' he'd said, 'somewhere.' Rose had this premonition, too. She couldn't wait to tell Luke about her day's adventures this evening. Once again she felt a great yearning to lean on him.

* * *

Rose left Hampstead at about 6 p.m. Much had happened to Gannet in the wilds of east Somerset in the past twelve hours that same day.

As she woke Gannet shook her wet coat and put her nose to the damp, golden leaf mould. The smells were acutely interesting in that beech wood — varied, conflicting, enticing, suspicious. A grey squirrel danced past her with a beech nut in its mouth, its bushy tail quivering delicately like a ballet dancer's dress. Forgetting her pregnancy and her lameness, Gannet tore after it: the squirrel accelerated; she was too slow; already it was scaling the trunk, and she was standing at the foot of the beech, reaching up the grey bark with her forepaws, yapping excitedly as if to say: 'I want you down here, not up there!' Six weeks ago, when she had hunted with her mate, Bandit, she had proved sharper than him. Now that she carried his pups and was in her third day without sustenance, he would have beaten her to the mark every time. Anyhow, squirrels had this tiresome habit of shooting up trees; she should concentrate on rabbits.

On the edge of the wood she found a rabbit, quite freshly killed, gutted, staked to the ground by a wire. Her mouth watered. But something must have triggered in her memory to remind her again of the day of the severed toes, when she had been in another pheasant-rearing copse. Full of circumspection, she left it severely alone. Not far away from that spot were three bantam's eggs with small squares removed from their shells. She passed her hypersensitive black nose across those and rejected them, too. Her judgement served her well. The eggs, intended for pheasant egg predators, magpies, jays and crows, were laced with strychnine. Had she eaten all three she might have suffered an excruciating death.

On she limped, ever eastward, not knowing whether the Utopia of her puppyhood was over the next rise or a million miles away, not knowing anything of time or space, having no expectations, only sensing that her true place was in that direction. The bad leg, the leg that had been hit by the motorbike, was on the mend now and she was beginning to use it properly. At about 4 o'clock, the rain set in again in the West Country. At about the same time that Rose was at the Dogs' Home, Gannet came to a cattle shed beyond the acres of corn, another man-made place that might mean food as well as shelter.

Three tom cats, sheltering from the drizzle, were curled up under a hay manger. Since earliest puppyhood Gannet had envisaged that everything furry and carried on four legs existed for one reason only, and that was to be chased by her. Forgetting hunger, pregnancy and friendlessness, she dashed straight at them, hackles menacing. It was one of the greatest mistakes she had yet made. The three toms, far from fleeing, but enjoying strength in numbers, unleashed such fury on her as she had never encountered in her life before. Ears flattened, coats all bushed, eyes flashing, claws bared, mouths spitting, they set on her in unison, as one creature, like a Medusa with three sets of teeth and sixty claws, scratching, kicking and yowling. And Gannet fought back.

These three young feral cats, litter-brothers, lived by their wits, marauding the farmland's wildlife. They were a menace to the local poultry farmer and gamekeeper alike. As Gannet found to her excruciating cost, they usually co-operated as a trio and when they met an enemy they were like hell let loose. Two full minutes elapsed before they disengaged and ran off, apparently deciding either that they had inflicted sufficient punishment or that they were not willing to share their cow-byre with an alien canine. Or perhaps because Gannet had split the ear of the largest of them and had given another a painful crunching bite over his back. This was the first time in those cats' lives that things had not quite gone all their way.

As for Gannet herself she looked as though she had been pulled at high speed through a thicket of African thorn bushes. The cats had raked her down both sides of her muzzle, yesterday's lameness was on her again and she was whimpering from the sheer shock of the mauling she had received. Not liking the place, she moved on, although the rain was still heavy, and quite soon found another small outlying farm building, this one half in ruins and standing on an eminence. To her delight she found, in a corner, two thick slices of white bread-and-butter, spread with fish paste, that had been left by picnickers. She bolted them ravenously, then fell to licking her wounds for several hours. The rain came down in torrents that night, and when dawn broke all the fields around were deeply flooded. Her ruined shed was like an island in the sea. Not having the strength or the inclination to swim, and anticipating that where human food had been human food might come again, she stayed there for the next three days. But, in that time, not another morsel passed her lips.

June 1

The day after Rose's visit Acland was at the bottom of his garden dead-heading daffodils when his next-door neighbour, David Young, gave him some news that was to shake him even more than when he first learned of Gannet's loss.

'I say, Trevor, I'm rather mystified by what you told me about that little dog of yours, I mean about it's going missing after chasing a cat in the early hours.'

Acland glanced up, quickly, suspiciously, with a sort of alarm in his eyes that men show when they think their secret doubts might be confirmed. 'Oh, yes, what's the trouble?'

'I didn't think anything of it at the time,' Young went on, 'but . . . now I remember you gave me the date as May 27th. Wasn't that the day Ruth went off to the West Country?'

'That's right, she went to stay with her sister in Devon.'

'Well, I happen to remember the date because I had to make an early start to catch a train for a board meeting in the north . . . I was shaving and drinking tea and I happened to be looking from my bedroom window down the avenue when Ruth drove off.'

'Oh, really, David?' said Acland, plucking at another group of dead daffodils, acting a nonchalance he didn't feel.

'And now I remember very distinctly seeing your little Batty looking out of the rear window.'

Acland stood up and faced his neighbour, saying nothing, only passing his tongue nervously between his dry lips.

Young shrugged. 'Well I suppose the dog could have gone missing later in the morning, if Ruth brought her back; but I understood you to say that it dashed out of the garage the moment she opened the door and wasn't seen again after that.'

'Yes, yes, that's right,' replied Acland, struggling to appear unmoved. 'Are you quite certain that Batty was in the back of Ruth's car?'

'Quite certain. Well, I must rush now. But I thought it might help if you knew . . . These wives, they can be very vague,' Young added with a carefree laugh as he turned away across his lawn.

The colour had drained from Acland's cheeks. Now he understood it all — Batty's collar on the motorway, her vanishing without trace from the neighbourhood, Ruth's evasiveness. It all added up.

What should he do? He still felt remorse for his own neglect of Batty. She had been a wonderful little companion. What could he do in atonement, he wondered as he made his way to the rubbish heap carrying, with an inordinately tight grip, the trugful of dead daffodils. He must do something to help Batty. That pretty blonde girl, Rose Maxwell, perhaps he should phone her.

'Yes, Rose Maxwell speaking . . .' he heard, and pangs of guilt were on him again. Batty was her dog. What did she call her? 'Gannet'. And his wife, Ruth, had deliberately abandoned the terrier — the dog that he had given her as a wedding anniversary present — at the other end of the country. This was terrible. 'Hallo, hallo, who is it?' He heard Rose's voice again.

'Oh, it's Trevor Acland — Hampstead — you called at our house about your dog.'

'Yes, I did. Are you going to tell me that she's turned up?' The question was carried in such girlish tones, so very excited. He felt a brute.

'No, I'm afraid not. But I've just discovered something . . . my Bat — your Gannet never ran away from here that morning. She was taken down to Somerset and deliberately discarded on the side of the motorway . . . Yes, as I say, that morning . . . No, I can't say who, we don't know. But I really think if you keep enquiring in that area . . . It goes without saying that she's yours if she's found . . . Oh, that's all right, it's a pleasure . . . Goodbye.'

Acland gazed blankly into space. That poor girl, she sounded so disappointed. No wonder: Batty was such a sweet dog, so full of character. But, God, how Ruth must've hated her! Would he face her with David Young's evidence? No, no, it wouldn't help. He had to try and heal, not aggravate the sores in their marriage. Only one thing was certain: there could be no more dogs at 3 Lime Glade. 'The curious thing is,' he thought to himself, 'I'd give all the tea in China to know what's become of the little creature. I bet she's alive somewhere. She's a survivor, if ever there was one.'

June 3

Gannet's instinct that where food was, food would come again deceived her. Those two fish paste sandwiches were an isolated chance.

Notwithstanding her poor condition, after three days her bad leg had unstiffened and was nearly mended. She was walking with her full weight on four again. The rain had stopped, too. With the floodwater subsided, that stream could be swum and her impulse said east, east, east to Elysium. Of course, if she had met Rose and identified her odour, her voice, her touch, she would have gone into paroxysms of joy, but the memory of Rose was hazy now. Gannet envisaged her only as the embodiment of love, warmth, security and happiness — an impersonal concept, an abstract environment, but still one that was essential to her well-being. In that quarter lay the heaven where Gannet and the family inside her must come to rest.

Since there had been no scavenging to be had around the farms and she was suffering more than she had ever suffered in her life from hunger, the urge to hunt and kill were hard upon her. She was famished to the point of desperation. She had chased a large number of rabbits this morning, only to see their bobbing scuts vanish like little balls of paper in a gale, down those maddening clay holes. If only she weren't weak and pregnant, if only those three fanatic cats hadn't closed one of her eyes with their deadly talons. The crimson scratches criss-crossing her body were hidden now by the orange clay of coney burrows. She persevered. Late in the afternoon she stalked a rabbit that could not have been more than six weeks old. It raced for a blackthorn hedge and, with Gannet only a few inches from its scut, in its panic it was slowed up by some briars. Hunger put Gannet at full stretch. In a trice her jaws were across its back and the tiny high-pitched squeals endured for less than a few seconds. Gannet rolled it over, sniffing every inch of it. She tore open the skin, her mouth filling with unwanted fur as she did so. In no time at all she was through to the succulent young flesh. Her muzzle, so recently bloodied by the cats, was now bloodied by the rabbit and she gorged until there seemed to be no room for more. Panting happily from heat as well as bodily gratification and the taste of the first fresh meat she had savoured since her morning's hunt in Bandit's company, she lay down beside her kill, swollen both from rabbit and pregnancy, the distension of her paunch contrasting with the thinness of her ribs and her general appearance of rough exposure. She was looking pear-shaped like a little red-and-white seal, a starved seal pup. This carcass was vitally important to her. She would keep it for another meal, carry it through the night, consume it in the morning. The taste and feel of it in her jaws reminded her blissfully of the halcyon Owlhurst days, and she would not let it go.

On she went, padsore and weary, with the rabbit's head swinging, its ears brushing the grass, but at a steady trot until about 10.30, when her head began to droop and her pace to slacken. She stumbled on a gravel drive that smelt strongly of dog. Not two canine smells, but three or four, the scent of each being quite distinctive. She dropped the rabbit carcass and sniffed around. From the smells emanated a feeling of harmony, the atmosphere seemed to be friendly. She picked up the tortured fur and flesh again and headed up the drive. In front of her, silhouetted in the radiance of the moon and flanked by the inky outlines of cedars of Lebanon, stood a Georgian house of red brick, square and sedate, its lights showing in bright vertical lines on the sides of its big, curtained sash window. Under the courtyard light shone three large cars, and, close by the wheels of one of them, a bone. It would be a refreshing change from rabbit. She dropped the carcass again and sniffed the bone, then pawed it tentatively, as a cat paws a mouse it has killed. Sensing it was wholesome she started chewing the gristle on its knuckle.

She had been gnawing for about ten minutes, when suddenly the heavy white front door opened, to throw out the lights of the hallway chandeliers to the forecourt light; and out came five men and four women, well fed and wined, the men in dinner jackets, the women in evening dresses with wraps around their shoulders. Gannet hesitated between the bone and the rabbit, then raised her hind legs in her habitual handstand and peed close to the bone, claiming its area as her territory. She left the bone and picked up the precious rabbit remains. Breaking into a canter she dashed past the festive group of people in the doorway and slunk into the shadows round the front corner of the house, a distance of fifty yards.

'Did you see that, Monica?' asked one of the women, whose flashing sequins had glinted in Gannet's eyes as she had dashed by. The other people faced the doorway saying their goodbyes to their hostess, the one they called Monica.

'See what?' In contrast to her glamorous women guests, Monica — a small bird-like person with twinkling, humorous features, in her late forties — wore no make-up and her dress was old and shapeless. She peered over the sequined shoulders. 'What was it?'

'A terrier, a smooth-coated terrier with what looked like a mangled baby rabbit in its mouth,' said the sequins.

'You don't have a Jack Russell, do you?'

'How extraordinary — no, I don't — which way did it go?'

'Round there!' The woman pointed. 'It looked a bit bedraggled.'

Monica adjusted her spectacles and peered again.

'Poor little devil, stray I suppose,' remarked one of the men, holding open the door of his Bentley as his wife got in.

'Doubtless it will take Monica over,' joked another. 'Ah, well, another dog'll make no difference one way or the other.' And there were peals of laughter while the last good-nights were said. 'Good-night, Monica . . . Good-night . . . Good-night.'

As Gannet heard the voices and ribaldry fade away and the cars crunch and purr down the drive, she was trotting across the expansive, well-trimmed lawn behind the house. She came to a summer-house with one of its doors hooked back. It smelt of warped cedar wood and the musty canvas of old deck chairs. She sniffed guardedly around the doors, then went in, dropped the carcass and started gnawing ravenously at it, cracking and eating the bones down to the ultimate morsel of marrow. Then she climbed a pile of cushions in a corner and, with the rabbit remains next to her, curled up in her tight circle. The injuries of the past week, added to exhaustion and pregnancy, allowed her only the lightest sleep. She heard the clock on the village church striking midnight and every hour after that, and every quarter, too. Until dawn. It would have meant nothing to her to know that her determined and traumatic trek had brought her close to the borders of Wiltshire and Hampshire, that she had crossed the river Avon at Downton and that the name of this place was Ripley Manor.

June 4

Hearing a quiet chorus of dog whimpers Gannet sat up, abruptly alert. Picking up her scent a trio of black-and-white springer spaniels, accompanied by a gold-coloured collie, bounded across the dew-drenched lawn towards the summer-house, to form a bristling, barking rank at its door. A human voice was behind them now. 'What is it, girls? What have you found?' exclaimed the woman who was addressed last night as Monica. 'Come away, then, let me take a look!'

Gannet stood her ground, giving full vent. She shuddered, with a blend of fury and fear. Here was hot-blooded, limb-tearing hostility. Here, too, came the dangerous vindictive species with feet that might kick and hands with prehensile claws that might clutch weapons with vicious intent. Here again came the terror of the two-legged species with big dogs trained to rip and kill, a terror threatening worse than ever. Could she slip out of this hut, and, in one hectic rush, escape between the rose-beds to the wilds beyond? Or would she be trapped within these close wooden walls? No, this time there could be no crazy bid for freedom. The five faces — four canine, one human — were too close to the door. Besides, the inhibiting weight and discomfort of her pregnancy were telling on her this morning, the abdominal pressure was throbbing to the extent that she knew, with her sharp terrier sense, that violent exercise would be very painful. She could only stand and attempt to hold this terribly threat at bay, protecting, if necessary, with her dying breath, the new life within her.

'Quiet, girls, quiet!' At those words the three spaniels and the collie were suddenly transformed. Now they sat in meek obedient attitudes on the lawn with angelic expressions in their eyes, as though the single aim of their lives was to please their mistress, who now placed a finger precisely on the bridge of her glasses. 'Ah, what clever girls to find this, aren't we?'

Gannet's frenzied trepidation of a moment ago was melted by the voice as a bitter night's snowfall melts under the radiance of the morning sun. Feeling the touch of the small sensitive hand between her ears she changed in a second from hypertense, hackle-stiff, noisy defiance to yielding, if apprehensive tail-wagging surrender. The woman's movements were as deft and careful as her clothes were careless, as her skirt was misshapen and rather threadbare, her tiny brogue shoes, scuffed, her stockings crumpled and her faded green husky torn in a dozen places.

Gannet rolled over on to her back now and the hand was on her ribs, the well-shaped fingers very gently massaging. 'Poor little terrier,' the soothing sing-song voice muttered, 'three-quarters starved and going to have a family quite soon by the look of it. . . Lovely sharp foxy head, nicely coupled, big kind intelligent eye, yes, all quality. Oh, but how thin, and all those puppies growing inside you and look, you've caught a rabbit, and in your condition. Clever bitch . . .' she muttered.

Monica Bowes-Onslow thought for a moment, then gave a nod of decision. 'All right, I'll look after you — until I find you another good home, so you needn't worry, and I'm going to call you 'Foxy', if that's all right? Now let me introduce you,' she continued, pointing to the spaniels: 'This is Boadicea, and these are her two daughters, Bundles and Bright. And this one,' she added, indicating the gingery collie, 'is Brandy. Mind if I pick you up, "Foxy"?' Gannet submitted almost fearlessly. Though the woman was short and slight in stature, her arms were strong and steady and protective. She seemed to cast a magician's soothing spell on all dogs. Those small arms held almost as much affection as Rose Maxwell's. While Gannet was carried towards the house, with its tall red Georgian proportions, the canine escort bobbed and surged and spoke around her with the jauntiness of a choppy sea menacing around a dinghy. And Gannet felt the shock-waves of their jealousy. Only Brandy, the golden collie, seemed not to regard her as a territorial usurper and rival.

They had reached a back porch festooned in wisteria with trunks as thick as a man's neck. Gently, Mrs Bowes-Onslow set her down on the kitchen floor. The kitchen was enormous — larger even than the sitting-room at 3 Lime Glade. The leftovers of the dinner-party lay all around. The smell of food set Gannet's mouth a-slaver. Despite her stomach's burden she jumped up and down, ravenously excited. The little woman opened a tin of dog meat, put half its contents in a bowl, poured on some boiling water and spooned it into a gravy. As Gannet whined, Mrs Bowes-Onslow mixed in a ladleful of dry meal, stirred it all together with the care of a chef making a Christmas pudding, ordered the other four to sit back, then placed the bowl on a stretch of newspaper. Gannet ate as though it was the first time in her life she had ever seen food. She only paused once and that was to give her throaty growl and ominous tail-shake when the two younger spaniels lurched at the bowl. Boady, their dam, kept her distance, regarding Gannet not with an unkindly expression but with one that seemed to question whether her mistress had gone out of her mind this morning thus to indulge such a whipper-snapper. Gannet licked the empty bowl frantically, as though if she licked hard enough, her tongue might rub away layers of its plastic to discover some more of that juicy protein beneath. Her tongue moved the bowl in arcs across the kitchen floor. Mrs Bowes-Onslow's lips turned up in a smile of wonder and amusement, as she prepared a second helping 'Ah, what a hungry little darling, then.'

She went to the kitchen telephone, looked up a number and dialled. 'It's Mrs Bowes-Onslow here, is Dr Jacklin there, please?'

Being told by his assistant who it was that wanted him, Dr Jacklin promptly left his client holding her yowling Siamese cat on the surgery table and, rubbing his hands on a towel, strode immediately to his desk. 'Good morning, Mrs Bowes-Onslow, how can I help you today?'

'A stray terrier has turned up here, pregnant, but otherwise all too thin, will you please come over.'

'Of course, what time?'

'Midday would suit me well.'

There was not another client on Dr Jacklin's list to whose home he would have driven to inspect their pregnant stray bitch, nor was there another whom he would have invited to name a time for an appointment. Clients waited in his waiting-room with their pets, sometimes long after their appointment time was due, and if they didn't like it they could go elsewhere. But the Honourable Mrs Bowes-Onslow was a client apart. Her late husband had been a Deputy Lieutenant and Chairman of the County Council, and now she, Monica Bowes-Onslow, was the owner of three thousand acres, not to mention two of Britain's top prize dairy herds. She was a principal judge at horse and dog shows, president of the county show and a magistrate to boot. Since her husband died and her children had been out in the world, her affections, as everyone knew, had been centred more and more on her animals. She might be small in physical appearance and gentle of manner but where animals were concerned she exercised the most important influence in the district.

'Of course — I shall be with you at midday,' said Dr Jacklin.

The vet arrived at Ripley Manor on the dot and was greeted with polite condescension by the butler, who had served the family of the late Honourable William Bowes-Onslow for nearly thirty years. Dr Jacklin was then conducted along the hall, through the blue drawing-room, through the library, through the green baize door, through the pantry and at last to the kitchen, where he found two daily women clearing up the last of the dinner things, four dogs that were familiar to him, side by side in baskets, and one that was not familiar — Gannet sitting on a bean bag with her new mistress kneeling beside her.

'Hello, thank you for coming out.' Monica Bowes-Onslow gave the vet a quick smile and lifted Gannet on to a table. She had a reputation for not wasting words. 'As you see, Foxy — that's the name I've given her — has had a rough time.' She fondled Gannet's ears while she spoke. 'How far gone do you think she is and are either she or her puppies in any danger?'

Dr Jacklin regarded Gannet from several angles, gave a careful push here and a pull there, made two quick tests and stood back, hand on chin. 'She's been through thick and thin by the look of her. Badly scratched and scarred, nasty abrasion on that leg . . . but there's nothing drastically wrong with her condition. H'm, I'd say she'd be having those pups in a fortnight.'

'Ah, well, that's a relief — I think I'll keep her in the summer-house where I found her. She obviously feels at home there and won't be disturbed by the others.'

'That sounds sensible. Well, nobody knows better than you how to cope,' replied Dr Jacklin.

'Would you care for a glass of sherry, or must you be rushing off to another appointment?' Mrs Bowes-Onslow thought that was the least she could offer having called the man out at such short notice.

'That would be most welcome.'

'Come along, then,' she said and reminded herself, as she led him through to the library, that she must remember to prepare Foxy's whelping-box in the summer-house. The sooner the little stray became used to her 'maternity ward' the better.

June 18

During this particularly wet summer no night was wetter or more turbulent than that of June 17th. Beginning soon after 9 o'clock, the storm opened with a series of thunderclaps interspersed with lightning as sharp and bright as battle, quickly breaking into torrential rain which drove against the summer-house with the passion of a heathen invader; and Gannet, ever-protective of the life in her womb, snarled her defiance at the tumult just as her own mother had done when she was born, as though it were an enemy host with a million fangs. But the doors and windows of this summer-house, unlike those of her dam's pen, resisted the rain, if not entirely the wind. The storm still raged full tilt at 3 o'clock in the morning, when Gannet, shivering from the draught, felt the abdominal pressures most acutely. Panting hard now she knew the moment of truth was imminent.

This pain and discomfort were in contrast to her treatment of the past fortnight, which had been as a blessing from heaven. Mrs Bowes-Onslow had allotted her this summer-house — this place of her own original instinctive choice that first night — all to herself with a comfortable, well-lined whelping-box in the corner. She had brought her four small meals a day and plenty of milk, and twice a day she had put her on a lead and taken her for gentle walks, while the three spaniels and the collie had played freely around her.

There was food in the opposite corner now, but Gannet didn't feel like eating. She felt weak and sick. Although her condition had apparently improved out of all recognition and she showed all the outward signs of good health, the traumas of the previous weeks had left emotional scars, while this thunder and relentless downpour did nothing to revive her morale.

The puppies started arriving soon after 3.30 at which time the storm ceased abruptly, giving way to a clear, quiet, balmy night. She bore down and the labour spasms began. The first pup protruded head first. She bit through the membranes, licked her firstborn frantically and, as the puppy sought her nipples, bit through the umbilical. The puppy was large, the effort almost intolerable. Gannet felt exhausted already, her head was hung low and she was panting urgently.

Mrs Bowes-Onslow had set her alarm for 5 o'clock, but thinking incessantly of Gannet, all alone in the storm, she had been unable to sleep. So, girded in gum boots, mackintosh and sou'wester and armed with a hurricane lamp she sloshed across the lawn at 3.40, reaching the summer-house at a critical moment, for Gannet's second pup came into the world as cold as the earth. Full of confident expertise Mrs Bowes-Onslow warmed her right hand, held the numb body up by its hind feet, and gently, but firmly rubbed it up and down. That was to no avail: it was stillborn. She sighed deeply and, wrapping it in a piece of newspaper, laid it against the opposite wall. After a torturingly long pause Gannet delivered her third and delivered it well. But its membranes were caught over its mouth and clearly she was too weak with pain and faintness to remove them, let alone bite through the umbilical cord or to eat its afterbirth as she had done with the first. Her eyes were dilated and her breath was coming in short sharp gasps. Mrs Bowes-Onslow acted with characteristic thoroughness. Having torn away the suffocating membranes, she took one of the pieces of cotton which she had brought with her from the house and tied it round the cord which she thus nipped away.

Giving birth to her fourth, Gannet suffered a breech. Seeing the pup's tiny claws peeping through the aperture, Mrs Bowes-Onslow caught them gingerly in the grip of her finger-nails and, by slow degrees, began to pull. After three or four minutes, kneading and coaxing, she had the body free and alive, but Gannet lay on her side as though at death's door. Nor was the night's work yet over. There was one more to come. Rather smaller than the others the fifth puppy came, full of life, wriggling and squeaking. 'A bitch . . . the runt of the litter,' Mrs Bowes-Onslow muttered to herself as she inspected it, then laid it alongside the others at Gannet's nipples. It was just sixty-three days since Gannet had been united with Bandit in Dick Saunders's yard, with the dreaded Mrs Slater standing by; sixty-three days; more of tragedy than triumph, more of woe than joy, days that had taken a heavier toll of both her body and spirit than anyone, even Dr Jacklin, could have detected.

It had been a long time since Mrs Bowes-Onslow had seen an animal quite so close to extinction as Gannet appeared now. Lying limply prostrate, the last breaths seemed to be ebbing from the terrier's racked body. How well does a dog of Gannet's intelligence remember? Humans' images of the past are said to be at their sharpest and most vivid in extremity. In

Gannet's anguish, an anguish in which consciousness was apparently almost eclipsed, did she recall the ecstatic rabbit-hunting days at Owlhurst with Rose, the person she had loved most in the world? Her breaths came slower still, they were almost invisible, contrasting with the lively suckling of her four blind infants.

What, if any, were her images? Was she remembering the day she led old Ted Jennings to the gravel pit where Rose lay immobile that winter's evening long ago? Or the dramatic morning of the Westdown's meet at the Queen of Spades? Or when Rose thrashed Leonard Trench that day at the kennels? Or when she, Gannet, had been stuffed into the sack by Trench and taken to Mrs Slater's? Did she remember the terrifying fox deep in the earth by the canal? Was she even now recalling those times with the Bryants, with Skipper and Bosun, the loneliness of Battersea, the friction of the Aclands, the adventures of her trek from the M5, which ended at this haven? Did her memory even trail back to the beginning — to the stormy night of her own birth?

The summer-house was lit with the grey light of dawn. As Mrs Bowes-Onslow extinguished her lamp a tear trickled down her cheek. Loving all animals she cried for the departure of her so recently found Foxy and she cried with a maternal sentimental joy, too, for the survival of the four lovely pups. But now that it was evident that Foxy was on the way out, how was she to cope with these orphans?

Dairy milk and a rubber teat? A bitch's milk, she recalled, contained twice as much fat as cow's milk! Must she get babies' milk, made up at double strength? She shook her head doubtfully, mournfully, then, of a sudden, she pulled herself together, removed her glasses, wiped away their mist, laid a blanket over Gannet's side, gathered up her things and crossed the lawn. She gave herself breakfast, then returned to the summer-house, saw that Gannet had not improved, and, soon after 7.30, was on to Dr Jacklin's private number.

'Good morning, sorry to bother you at this unearthly hour . . . Yes, four out of five are alive and well, but I'm afraid there's no hope for the dam . . . Yes, I did check — two dogs and two bitches, the last bitch was appreciably smaller than the others . . . It was terrible for poor Foxy, as you can imagine.'

'I'm so sorry to hear about the bitch . . . Must have had a tougher time on her own than we thought . . . She's met her

Waterloo . . . Yes, well it's actually June 18th, Waterloo Day. By the way, do you know that old superstitious rhyme about the runt of the litter?'

'I can't say I do Dr Jacklin.'

'So far as I remember it goes like this: "When pups are born on a stormy night, Life is going to be cruel and bitter, Life is going to be one long fight, For the smallest one, the runt of the litter." It's a well-known bit of doggy folklore among the old countrymen.'

'Is that so? Well, fortunately for the runt the storm had stopped by the time Foxy gave birth. Can you come round as soon as possible and advise on the puppies?'

'Yes, of course, Mrs Bowes-Onslow, I'll be over right away . . . And perhaps we could discuss the charity party at the same time?'

'Charity party?'

'The do at Ripley Manor on August 3rd. There's no problem about it, I hope?'

'No, no, of course not — the cocktail party. Yes, we'll talk about that, too. I'd quite forgotten about it in the heat of the moment.'

Oh, dear, she thought, there's so much to contend with. What was it in aid of? The Home of Rest for Horses. A cocktail party here at Ripley of all things, caterers and tents and goodness knows what else. And who cajoled her into it? Dr Jacklin, of course, blast him! And now . . . now, poor Foxy had to be disposed of. Another death, another burial.

'Are you there, Mrs Bowes-Onslow?'

'Yes, I'm here.'

'August 3rd. The invitations really ought to go out within a couple of weeks.'

'Yes, certainly. They should arrive from the printers any moment. I'm sorry to be so vague. I'm so upset about Foxy.'

Dr Jacklin paused. 'Well, while there's life there's hope. Next thing we know you'll be entering her for the terrier show.'

'Oh? When's that?'

'It's part of the County Show on September 1st.'

'Foxy would do well at that.'

The vet let out another restrained laugh. 'Yes — but if you'll forgive my saying so — I can't somehow envisage you there.'

'Can't you indeed!'

'Mrs Bowes-Onslow, I'll give £100 to any of your animal charities you like to name for the pleasure of seeing you show that terrier.'

'In which case I'll do it . . . if she lives, which I doubt.'

CHAPTER SEVEN

'Are those both Monica's dogs?' asked the man in the neat grey pin-stripe, pointing between the champagne-sipping groups towards the space that separated the garlanded white marquees.

'They are indeed,' replied Claudia Fairley, the woman whose sequins had flashed in Gannet's eyes the night she staggered up Ripley Manor's long drive. 'The goldy-brown one, the collie, is Brandy — surely you know Brandy, Michael? As a matter of fact I can tell you about the other one, too,' continued Mrs Fairley, taking a canapé from the tray proffered by the caterer's maid. 'It turned up thin as a rake and carrying a young rabbit in its mouth when we were on the point of leaving a dinner-party of Monica's in early June. Monica, being Monica, promptly adopted it, then fattened it and cosseted it as only she can, and lo and behold within a couple of weeks it gave birth to four perfectly good puppies, if you please.'

'It's looking in the pink now,' said the man in pin-stripe watching Brandy and Gannet cavorting round the guy ropes.

' "Foxy", she calls it. Made an astonishing recovery. Monica told me it seemed like a dead dog when its young arrived. In fact she informed the vet it couldn't possibly survive. But by the time he arrived on the scene, it had rallied and was giving milk as happy as could be. You really ought to see the pups, they're too adorable — but I'm afraid she'll get rid of them all. 'Ah, here she is now . . . What a marvellous get-together this is, Monica. I hope it's going to raise lots of money for the charity.'

Monica Bowes-Onslow, who never felt natural in party clothes, pulled on the uneven hem of her yellow cotton dress, which contrasted sadly with Mrs Fairley's impeccably cool blue that sultry evening. 'Well, I was worried about the price of the tickets — £10. Yet a hundred and fifty people have come, would you believe it? Dr Jacklin assured me that people will pay anything to be seen in the right company.'

'How right he was!' agreed Mrs Fairley. 'I was just saying what an incredible recovery your adopted terrier's made.'

'Foxy? The toughest little animal I've ever known.'

'Will you keep her?'

'Of course I shall keep Foxy, having nursed her through that crisis. No one has claimed her, although my brother has taken a great fancy to her. He even asked if he could have her.'

Michael Lonsdale raised his eyebrows. 'Your brother the vicar?'

'Yes, Richard,' replied Mrs Bowes-Onslow flatly.

'He doesn't look much of a doggie man to me.'

Mrs Bowes-Onslow gave a regretful smile. 'Well, no. He's so lazy about exercising himself, he lives a very sedentary life; a dog might do him a lot of good. But naturally I wouldn't dream of surrendering her to anyone . . . Ah, there is Richard, he's picked Foxy up. It looks as though he's coming over . . . Richard, have you met Claudia Fairley, Michael Lonsdale? — my brother Richard Illingworth.'

The Reverend Richard, a rotund amiable-looking man, shuffled across the lawn in short steps with feet that pointed outwards, took a greedy handful of canapés from a caterer's tray, nodded to the other two, then beamed on Gannet, who was cradled in his church-black arm. 'Isn't she a lovely little thing? Angelic face.' But the vicar was obliged to use his free hand to hold Gannet by the scruff now. She was craning, ears pricked, over his elbow, eyes following every movement of her new intimate Brandy, who was playing with the three spaniels on the fringe of the party. She was struggling to escape the vicar. There was nothing she wanted more than to be with her friends. Besides, the Reverend Richard smelt alien, his vibrations did not really atune with dogs.

Richard Illingworth turned to his sister. 'I do wish you'd let me have her, Monica.'

'Not on your life! The next thing on Foxy's programme is the County Show.'

Mrs Fairley sipped her champagne and said, 'I didn't know there was a dog section there.'

'I've entered her for the terrier races and also the Jack Russell classes,' said Mrs Bowes-Onslow. 'The vet's offered a wager of £100 for any charity I choose if I'll do it, and — you know me — I can't refuse a challenge!'

Mrs Fairley laid a hand on Gannet's craning neck. 'I don't see how any judge could possibly resist her.'

'Indeed not,' agreed Michael Lonsdale. 'She hasn't got a blemish except for her missing claws; I'm afraid she'd get marked down for those.'

'She's so perfect in every other respect I'm hoping the judge'll overlook that,' Mrs Bowes-Onslow replied. 'It's to be Derek Fowles, who judges terriers all over the south. I happen to have done a lot for him. He sits on one of my committees . . . Anyhow, I must move on now, I have to draw the raffle. I think we ought to make another couple of hundred on the raffle. Oh, do put Foxy down, Richard, she hates being mollycoddled.'

When the vicar gave his seraphic smile and did as he was told, Gannet dashed like lightning to rejoin Brandy, and, in celebration at being reunited, they ran circles round each other and tripped up smart ladies who were clenching raffle tickets and trying to listen to the winning numbers.

August 23

As the days went by Gannet spent less and less time with her brood, although she was still attached to them all, especially her last born. Monica Bowes-Onslow had already promised three of the puppies, and only the runt of the litter was still to be claimed. So far no one wanted it. Albeit the smallest, it was quite the most courageous and at times in sheer self-defence against its superior brothers and sisters, almost looked like being top dog.

These were great days for Gannet. In fine weather she was always out playing and jousting with Brandy and the three spaniels or simply sunning herself. Brandy had formed a close attachment with the puppies and was now sleeping in the summer-house, too; Gannet rejoiced in Brandy's company. As for Mrs Bowes-Onslow, she was essentially an outdoor woman who believed in plenty of exercise for her dogs, never less than an hour and a half a day and never on leads. She enjoyed a high respect as a breeder of gun dogs. Boady, Bundles and Bright were all good workers and Mrs Bowes-Onslow, who had never wanted to carry a gun herself, nevertheless did a lot of 'picking-up' at the local shoots during the pheasant season. She always claimed her 'picking-up' was the closest involvement anyone could enjoy with a dog, and despite the views of other serious gun-dog owners, who insisted that rabbit-hunting was ruinous to discipline, she let hers hunt rabbits out of the shooting season to their hearts' content. On these occasions Gannet would give chase in tandem with the collie, while the spaniels hunted as a trio. Gannet and Brandy, in their affinity, always seemed to be in the same mood at the same time, whether it was for hunting or junketing or just for resting.

One afternoon towards the end of August marked the tragic end to this happy phase of Gannet's life, caused by a man called Jake Bristow. Bristow kept goats in an orchard adjacent to the Ripley estate, and was obsessed with the notion that his goats were being frequently worried by dogs.

Mrs Bowes-Onslow was exercising her dogs on Bristow's side of her estate that afternoon when she heard a shot in the direction of the orchard. This was quickly followed by a second shot, but Gannet and the collie were out of sight. A fit and athletic woman, she sprinted towards the reports, arriving at the orchard fence in time to witness the closing scene of the catastrophe.

Brandy lay grotesquely dead, her golden fur spattered with blood, at least twenty yards on Mrs Bowes-Onslow's side of the fence. Gannet, crazy with rage and growling continuously, had Bristow by the trouser leg. He was sitting propped against the orchard's post-and-rails clutching an ankle with both hands and with a look of excruciating pain on his face. His gun was lying on the grass, breech open, three or four yards away. Mrs Bowes-Onslow grasped the situation immediately. When Brandy was shot Gannet must have gone straight for the man, and tripped him up with such a jerk that he fired the second barrel in the air, letting go of his gun as he went sprawling on his ankle. Gannet, detesting her friend's murderer, went on tugging at his trouser-leg with a good deal more ferocity than she was accustomed even to show a predator in a hole, and Mrs Bowes-Onslow was fuming with a rage that almost matched Gannet's. But it was useless to remonstrate with a man so preoccupied with his own pain. As Gannet was doing a magnificent job and Bristow was obviously unable to move, she went straight to the nearest call-box and dialled 999.

The police and an ambulance arrived quickly. The evidence was there for all to see. Bristow tried to claim he had shot Brandy in the orchard worrying his goats and that Mrs Bowes-Onslow had moved the carcass outside. But the blood on the grass all round the dead dog disproved the killer and Mrs Bowes-Onslow had no hesitation in deciding to bring a charge against him. With the arrival of the police, Gannet abandoned the trouser-leg, went across to Brandy's body and lay close to it, whining and shivering disconsolately. She even tried to prevent Mrs Bowes-Onslow from picking it up.

The returning party, led by Mrs Bowes-Onslow, holding Brandy's mangled body wrapped in a cloth she had borrowed from the ambulance, presented a dismal little cavalcade — one dead collie and her four devoted companions in procession. The spaniels slouched along, heads hung low, while Gannet's occasional whining never failed to bring a fresh lump to Mrs Bowes-Onslow's throat.

Brandy was buried at the bottom of Ripley Manor's garden, the sixth grave and miniature headstone on that hallowed ground, and for nearly a week Gannet paid pilgrimages to the little mound, lying across it, whimpering.

* * *

By the time of the County Show on September 1st, Gannet was just about back in condition and in a reasonable state of morale. Not being accustomed to the grooming preparatory to a show, Gannet did not at all enjoy such attention, although the sequence of the session became progressively less irksome. For Mrs Bowes-Onslow began with the hard brush, advanced to a soft one and finished with a piece of chamois-leather. Being used to brushing spaniels she was inclined to go a sight too hard on Gannet's short, thin coat, and Gannet was most relieved when it was over and she was in the car and on the way to the County Show, blissfully ignorant of the fact there would be another grooming session when she got there.

Unfortunately, there were so many Jack Russell classes, seventeen in all, that some of them — including Gannet's, which was to be simply for 'the best smooth-coated bitch' — had to be postponed until after the races. Mrs Bowes-Onslow, who had no previous experience of terrier shows, was most upset about this as it meant she would have little time to tidy up her Foxy after the hurly-burly of the races. So that day Gannet raced first and entered the show ring second, and the beginning of the afternoon was all triumph for Mrs Bowes-Onslow, if not for Gannet.

Enclosed by sheep wire the terrier racecourse measured some fifty yards. The bait was a fox's brush dragged along the ground by a system of wires and wheels. At the starting-point was a trap composed of six adjacent boxes with six doors behind and a single wire-mesh door in front. The entries were dressed in coloured woollen identification collars: Gannet's colour was blue. Never having experienced anything remotely like this before she was nervous when Mrs Bowes-Onslow placed her in the box for which she had been drawn. The bustle of the organisers and other owners and spectators frightened her, as did their shouts of *Snip! Bertie! Patch! Towler!* and the barking and whimpering of animation on this side and that.

Mrs Bowes-Onslow had moved up to the finishing-point and Gannet singled out her cultivated voice calling *Foxy! Foxy!* among the cacophony of other exhortations. Gannet squealed and her five rivals squealed, too, as the prelude to the start of the race increased its crescendo. It had been a long time since she had seen a fox's brush and the sight of it stirred thrilling recollections. To arouse the competitors' blood even further the man who worked the machine caused the white-tagged tail to jerk back and forth. None of the contestants was keener to have a go at it that Gannet; she threw herself against the wire in paroxysms of hunt-terrier craving.

When the starter pulled the handle and the trap door snapped up, the six terriers shot forward like dogs out of Hades. 'Foxy! Foxy! Come on, Foxy!' sounded Mrs Bowes-Onslow's accent among the shouts of 'Get movin', will yer, Patch!' and ''Urry, old Towler!' But Gannet didn't hear her voice now. Every degree of every faculty she possessed, every fibre in her muscular body was concentrated on that furry lure. She cared nothing for the prestige of the race that concerned her mistress and the rest of the crowd. She had to gain possession of the brush entirely for its own sake. Almost from the start she was two lengths ahead of any of the others. To her intense frustration, however, the brush vanished down a length of drainpipe, and while her competitors were finishing the race and squabbling in the enclosures, she was yapping furiously at the pipe's maddening aperture.

'Blue first!' shouted the finishing judge, holding up a blue disc. Mrs Bowes-Onslow picked Gannet up and patted her congratulations on her quivering shoulder. The four heat winners went on to the final; Gannet wore yellow this time. She repeated her success, winning the championship cup and the red rosette. 'Yellow's the winner!' was heard on every side. But the glory was lost on her. Amid admiring cries of 'Did you ever see anything like the pace of that little tyke?' and 'Coo, what a flyer!' and 'Bet that one's 'ad a bit of fox experience!' Gannet just went on growling and scratching at that annoying drain-pipe eclipsing the seductive russet tail. And to make matters worse, Mrs Bowes-Onslow, intent on repeating her success in the show ring, then gave her another five minutes of vigorous grooming.

Most of the other classes had been judged — 'best rough or broken-coated dog', 'best Jack Russell-type family pet', 'best bitch puppy', 'best veteran over six years', 'best at twelve inches and under', 'best progeny', and others besides. Now it was the turn of the 'smooth-coated bitch' class.

Swelled with pride from the races Mrs Bowes-Onslow paraded Gannet round the show-ring almost as though it was a foregone conclusion she would win. Catching the eye of the judge, Derek Fowles, sallow, thin lipped, she gave a twinkling, confidential grin. Fowles, seeing her as an unexpected candidate to be showing a terrier, returned it with an eyebrow-raising smile. On his command they lined up in a single rank. He inspected each terrier with professional care — he lifted their ears, measured their girths, attested their depth through the heart and ribs, examined their eyes and appraised their general presence.

Having gone through all those motions with Gannet — whose quality and bearing despite her small proportions, stood, squarely above the other eleven — he peered at the foot with the missing toes and, almost imperceptibly, gave a headshake of regret. 'Oh, surely you're not going to mark her down on -' Mrs Bowes-Onslow began. But with a sharp steely look Derek Fowles cut her short. Then some memory seemed to dawn on the man. He looked at Gannet again, frowned quizzically, glanced back for a moment at Mrs Bowes-Onslow, then proceeded to the next terrier.

An assistant approached nine owners, including Mrs Bowes-Onslow, politely asking them to remove their dogs from the ring. It was on her lips to say 'Surely you don't mean us?' but she checked herself and left the ring with a grace that scarcely betrayed her disappointment. Three competitors remained to be judged for the red, blue and green. As for Gannet, having set eyes on one fox's brush at this show, her heart had been fixed on one thing only — to find another. The disappointed Monica Bowes-Onslow was on the point of leaving the area when she heard her name called from behind. It was Derek Fowles.

'How are you, Monica? Sorry there was no prize for yours.'

'So am I,' replied Mrs Bowes-Onslow with a tight little smile.

'She's impeccable in every respect — but for that one blemish on her foot . . . Er, what I really wanted to say is that I've met her before.'

Mrs Bowes-Onslow gave him a look of surprise. 'Oh, really, where?'

'She was in the Westdown hunt kennels. You know — Owlhurst. Belonged to a pretty, fair girl there called Rose Maxwell. I'd heard she'd lost her. I'd be most intrigued to know how you came by her?'

'Well, I must confess she turned up on my doorstep as a stray. But how can you be certain she's the same one?' Mrs Bowes-Onslow continued to gaze at the man with an expression of total disbelief.

'There's no doubt about it. I see hundreds of terriers every year. There aren't many I wouldn't recognise a second time.' He scrutinised Gannet again. 'The markings, the conformation, and particularly the missing claws, she stands out absolutely on her own. "Gannet" was the name Rose Maxwell gave her.'

Mrs Bowes-Onslow frowned; she was silent for a moment or two. What was racing through her mind was a yearning for some confirmation that Fowles was mistaken and, if he was right, the problem of how to avoid relinquishing this little dog she had come to love. Gannet's devoted brown eyes looked up towards hers, while her stumpy tail switched apprehensively. Mrs Bowes-Onslow felt a lump in her throat. Supposing this Maxwell girl wanted her back? It didn't bear thinking about. She turned from Gannet to Fowles with a dubious look. 'The Westdown hunt kennels must be all of eighty miles from here. I hardly think it possible that Foxy can be the one you're thinking of.'

But Fowles was adamant. 'Monica, I'm absolutely certain of it. Anyhow, there are all sorts of ways in which she could have turned up at Ripley. I hate to say it, but I think you ought to make contact with Rose Maxwell.'

Mrs Bowes-Onslow gave a deep sigh. 'Look, Derek, will you do me a great favour?'

'I'll try.'

'Well, you know the girl, and what I'm wondering is . . . would you be very kind and ring her for me and give her my number.'

'All right.'

Mrs Bowes-Onslow glanced nervously at her wristwatch. 'Well, now, I have to judge the shire horses at 4.30.' And with an impatient 'Foxy! Come on Foxy!' and hiding the emotion in her eyes she turned on her heel and strode quickly across the showground, thinking that at any rate, she would keep Foxy's last remaining puppy.

'I'll be in touch,' Derek Fowles called at her back.

As Mrs Bowes-Onslow registered that message she remembered a small compensation. Dr Jacklin has lost his bet. He'd have to pay her a hundred pounds. Marvellous!

September 2

'Who's that then?' asked Ted Jennings perching on the kennels office stool and taking his well-chewed pipe from his mouth. Screwing up his face he pressed the receiver hard against his ear, hearing the telephone voice as though it came from the opposite end of the world. 'Oh, Mr Fowles, hallo, sir . . . Ay, she still work's here, only she ain't called Rose Maxwell no more, she's called Rose Peterson. She's on her honeymoon an' all, she'll be back in ten days . . . What's that? Can you say it again, please, bit hard of hearing . . . No . . . *No,* I can't believe it, I don't, not Gannet! You can blow me down with a feather. Cor, Rosie'll be over the moon! . . . No, I ain't in touch with her . . . Eh? That's the other side of Wiltshire, ain't it? . . . No, I don't drive further nowadays 'n it takes to pick up a carcass or load o' straw. But Rose'll get across soon enough when she hears her Gannet's live and well, you won't see her for dust; she'd be on the next flight to Japan if it meant getting that little bitch back. She'll be home on the 11th to be exact . . .'

When Ted replaced the receiver he stood shaking his head and smiling for a full minute. Then he muttered: 'Gannet alive and kicking, just wait until I tell the missus!'

* * *

The telephone rang at Ripley Manor a few minutes later. 'Mrs Bowes-Onslow speaking . . . Hallo, Derek . . . On her honeymoon, back in ten days? I see . . . Hold on, Derek, I've got my brother Richard staying here, he's trying to say something.' Mrs Bowes-Onslow placed her hand over the mouthpiece and snapped: 'Go and sit down, Richard, and wait till I've finished.' The Reverend Richard Illingworth, rather sulkily doing as he was told, released struggling Gannet from the crook of his elbow. She promptly leaped towards the three spaniels who made their pattern of black-and-white on the carpet.

'Yes, that's all right, Derek, tell her to ring me as soon as she returns. She can pick Foxy up by arrangement any time she likes and will you tell her there's one of Foxy's puppies left, and that I'd like to keep that. Yes . . . Goodbye, Derek.' Ringing off she turned impatiently to her brother 'Now, Richard, what *is* it?'

'I was wondering whether I couldn't get Foxy back to the girl.'

'Well, you might, but as you heard she'll not be back for ten days and you're heading home for Guildford tomorrow.'

'Can you show me on the map where the Owlhurst kennels are?'

Mrs Bowes-Onslow opened a road atlas and followed the route east with her forefinger. 'There,' she pointed.

'That couldn't be more than fifteen minutes run from Guildford.'

'Less than that probably.'

'Well, why not let me drop Foxy off with the kennelman tomorrow? That'd save a lot of trouble all round.'

Monica Bowes-Onslow smiled indulgently at her brother. 'Can I trust you not to lose her?'

'Of course you can.'

'Well, now, I suggest you go out and get some fresh air. You've been indoors all day.'

'Oh, don't be tiresome, Monica. You know the one thing I simply hate is fresh air. What time's dinner?'

September 3

The next day was sparkling autumn with two glorious wild walks for Gannet and her spaniel friends. Most of the rest of it was spent playing with her remaining puppy, or gambolling after the rabbits living among the acres of rhododendrons at the bottom of Ripley's south garden, or browsing on the lawns. The spaniels now filled the place in Gannet's heart vacated by poor Brandy. The three of them looked very beautiful as they sat up on Ripley's impeccable lawns with the breeze dancing through their curly black-and-white coats, fanning their long black ears. Gannet had been a part of their happy coterie for so long.

Boady, Bundles and Bright now squatted on the gravelled courtyard gazing up at Gannet with those particular expressions of sadness that are almost exclusive to the spaniel breed. Perhaps it was something transmitted from their mistress's demeanour that the three of them knew, or seemed to know, that their little companion of three months standing was leaving them for a long time. Gannet herself, tucked in the corpulent Reverend Richard's arms, obviously felt no such intuition, for she looked back at the three piebald figures, if not exactly brimming with joy, then at least quite confidently, as if to say: 'Just hang on a minute till I free myself from this black smelly arm and I'll be romping on the lawn with you and then I'll be going on to the summer-house to check on my puppy.' But when she was released from the vicar's arms, it was to be pushed on to the rear seat of his old Morris. There was no escaping that car.

The Reverend Richard closed the driver's door, rolled down the window and gave his sister his apple-cheek smile. '*Au revoir*, Monica.'

'Be sure to ring the kennels as soon as you're home and fix a time with their man. Don't forget he's called Jennings. You've got his number.'

'Of course. Goodbye.'

With that Richard Illingworth rolled up the driver's window, let in the clutch and crunched his Morris over the courtyard gravel.

Gannet leaped up to the rear window and gazed back towards Ripley Manor's portico The spaniels remained squatting in their rank of three, their eyes following the car down the drive in sad wonder. Gannet's multiple bark, however, was quite buoyant. 'Hold on, you three,' it seemed to be telling them, 'I'll be out of this machine in a moment and right by your side.'

But the car rolled on down the three hundred yards'

length of drive, past the cedars, between the tall stone piers and wrought-iron gates that marked the entrance to Ripley and so out on to the tarmac and the roads leading east-north-east to Guildford. Gannet lay prone against the rear window and, with her chin resting between her forepaws, emitted her most melancholy whine, as though at last understanding that she was irrevocably trapped, taken away from her spaniel companions, separated from the last of her puppies.

Gannet lay resignedly by the window, but as the journey wore on a different sensation began to dawn on her. The old yearning forgotten these last three months, and prompted by a new unhappiness, swept over her again. This vehicle was heading in the direction of her first home. And with that perception came a faint, sweet memory of Rose.

The Reverend Richard Illingworth had toyed on and off for several years with the idea of keeping a dog, of what he called 'a convenient size and temperament', but he had always ended up banishing the notion from his head on the grounds that — being deeply preoccupied with and immersed in the affairs of his parish — he would not be able to cope. But now, with this delightful, cuddlesome little creature in his temporary possession, a fresh opportunity presented itself. If, instead of surrendering Foxy to the kennels today, or even tomorrow, he were to keep her until young Mrs Peterson returned, he would have a good chance to get accustomed to a dog — 'to see whether dog ownership really suits my lifestyle,' he said to himself. After all, it wouldn't matter to the girl where Foxy spent the next ten days.

Having thought this enterprising scheme over for twenty minutes or so, he rattled his fingernails on the steering-wheel, looked at Gannet in his driving mirror and gave a small nod. There — his mind was made up. He'd buy a collar and lead and some tins of dog meat and a rubber bone and a nice compact wicker basket with a deep soft cushion and . . . oh, yes, as autumn seemed to be coming on extra cold this year, a little woollen coat to put on when she was let out to relieve herself. Then, if he went ahead and acquired a dog of his very own, which he probably would now, it would be entirely equipped in advance.

'Foxy — are you there?' he called over his shoulder as he approached Guildford. 'You're going to have ten days holiday with Uncle Richard, you lucky little thing!'

September 13

It was Saturday morning. Not that Gannet noticed much difference from any other day. She had spent 95 per cent of her time during the past ten days in a little wicker basket — lined with layers of soft blankets below a cushion — that stood in the corner of the vicarage sitting-room. The Reverend Richard Illingworth kept his central heating at a steady 80 degrees. Hot and airless and lonely that sitting-room was for Gannet, like a sumptuous prison cell. During her first two or three days in this new house she had yearned for the life at Ripley Manor and the company of her recent soul-mates. She had whined to be taken out; she had jumped up suggestively at her lead which hung in the hall and, hopelessly and longingly, she had scratched at the front door. And, whenever the vicar appeared, she had jumped up and down and around his knees with expectant yelps.

She felt the old urge for reunion with the last state of happiness she had known, with Mrs Bowes-Onslow and the three spaniels and the whole environment of Ripley Manor. Yet there was a confusion in her russet-and-white head between Ripley and Owlhurst. On the second day she had slipped past the vicar's daily cleaner, when that none-too-friendly woman had left the front door open one morning. Gannet's orientation being accurate as ever, she had trotted eastwards, threading her way through the Guildford streets ever on the Owlhurst bearing. She had reached the suburbs by the time a family of ardent dog-lovers, suspecting her to be a stray, cornered her, bewildered her into submission, put her in their car and drove her to the nearest police station. Illingworth soon reclaimed her, and from that hour forward she was shut up more closely than ever.

Within another couple of days she resigned herself to the knowledge that the vicar never went for walks and that, in this new life, all she would ever see of the outside world would be, twice a day, his patch of garden, and that only for a few minutes on the lead with a tiresome little woollen coat taped round her body. It was now clear that the vicar's daily cleaner positively disliked dogs and Gannet detested the daily cleaner. Whenever she was in the room, they contrived totally to ignore one another. She was fed sumptuously twice a day while tedium, monotony and idleness brought on the desire to eat twice as much as was good for her.

Getting fatter than she had ever been, she lay nearly all day in a state of torpor in the basket, curled in her turgid sausage, nose powder-dry, caring nothing for the world outside of herself, as though hibernating out the last stretch of her life. After six days her yearning for those palmy days of high summer with Mrs Bowes-Onslow, Boady, Bundles and Bright, died as the embers of a fire. But, whenever the vicar entered the room she would suddenly come to, desperate for distraction, and knowing that the only diversion she could hope for from him was either the feel of his big fingers in her coat, or food, she would waddle to one of the cupboards where her titbits were kept and whine. And the vicar, being a glutton, would gratify her with a rotund smile of fellow-feeling and a handful or two from one of the packets, a dozen more so-called 'liver squares' or 'beef chunks', 'chocolate pastilles' or 'bonemarrow rolls'.

At 8.15 the Reverend Richard pulled the armchair close to Gannet's wicker basket, and with the demeanour of one offering the last sacraments, prepared to say goodbye to her. As he gazed on her he began to wonder whether he ought to have taken her for a little further each day than the bottom of his tiny garden — a saunter down to the street corner and back, perhaps? And as he pondered on the possibility of that neglect his guilt began to grow.

He had regarded Foxy's welfare subjectively, had given her the sort of existence he would have liked had he been a dog, instead of the open-air life a young terrier cherished. Swiftly, in these farewell moments, he became, as he put it to himself, 'starkly conscious of my neglect of this creature of God's, of my culpability'. Then he wondered for a few minutes how he could atone for that negligence. He made a snap decision, an irrational decision not uncharacteristic of the man. He would show what he could do when he really put his mind to it. The spirit would now prevail over the flesh. He would compensate in small measure for the wrong he had done Foxy — by giving her a wonderful last walk on Raynham Common. He had often heard it said that that was where Guildford people walked their dogs. He would be back by 9.30. That was only half an hour later than the appointed time. The girl wouldn't mind waiting. She'd be glad to know that her little terrier dog had received proper exercise before it was passed back to her.

* * *

Rose knocked on the vicarage door in the very moments that the parish church was striking nine. The vicar's daily cleaner answered.

'I've come to see Mr Illingworth.'

''Fraid he's out, miss, out walkin' the little dog.'

Rose frowned. 'Oh, but I definitely had an appointment with him for nine.'

'You Mrs Peterson then?'

'That's right,' said Rose with confidence though she was only just getting used to the change from Maxwell to Peterson.

'Well, he said he was expecting you, dear, but there's something been on his mind this morning like. First he says he's waiting in for you, then he says it'll have to be later. An hour ago or thereabouts he ups and put on all his clobber and the dog's little coat and all and goes out. Quite unlike the vicar it is, never goes out much, least of all to the countryside. Said he was going on the common.'

'On the *common!*' Rose repeated.

'That's right, miss, Raynham Common. He says I'm to show you his living-room where you'd be quite cosy till he comes back.'

'Well, I haven't got much choice, have I?'

'You haven't, neither,' said the daily help, ushering Rose into that hall in which Gannet had whined for hours on end to be let out. 'And I'll tell you another thing', added the woman, 'I'm right glad you're taking the little perisher away; a dog don't seem right with Mr Illingworth, don't seem right at the vicarage. I hope he's learned his lesson this last week.'

* * *

Wrapped up like a funeral mummy in his voluminous black overcoat, scarf, gloves and shiny goloshes and with his black hat pulled well down to his ears, the Reverend Richard looked quite incongruous on the wild common. There was a strong wind. He found little to commend the brisk air and the muddy pathways, drew no comfort from the windswept bracken, the leaf-dropping silver birches or the needle-dark spruces. For him Mother Nature's face was really rather bleak and inhospitable. Nor did Gannet — in her black woollen coat, prettily trimmed with green — look the part. She resembled more a pet prize pony rugged up and led out on a winter's morning than the tough and resolute scion of an ancient strain of working terriers. The vicar had never found her more difficult than now. How she longed for freedom, how she had resented those last ten days of imprisonment. She pulled relentlessly on her lead, leaned into her collar as though she would strangle herself and kept snuffling at the ground. She dragged and jerked and irritated the vicar as she had never irritated him before.

'Now, Foxy,' he mumbled, raising an admonitory finger of his free hand. 'What is it your nose finds so fascinating on this bland landscape, I wonder? What is all the sniffing about? Foxy! Stop this pulling at once! I don't at all approve of your dictating our pace, do you understand? Oh, all right then, you are the victor, Foxy — I'm going to let you off the lead. But you're not to run away, is that clear? You're to stay close to me. We have to go back to Rose Peterson in a moment. Now you're loose — but *heel!*'

What was *that?* Gannet's expression was saying. Fully woken from her comatose state and disregarding the man talking to her, she pricked her ears, trotted forward a few paces, then stopped abruptly, one forepaw raised in anticipation, poised like a sculptor's model. The distant echo was tantalisingly familiar. She pranced forward, away from the vicar, deep into the autumnal bracken and heather, until she came to a clearing where she stopped again, straining to distinguish the far-off reminiscent sound. Its rhapsody was interrupted by her erstwhile master's petulant call: 'Come *here*, Foxy, I say! Heel!'

Her ears flattened resentfully on her neck at the command, then they switched this way and that, straining to pick up the enticing melody beyond. Her woollen coat, being caught in the brambles, went askew, its tapes were loose. She was at least three hundred yards from the vicar now, but she could hear his futile whistle and again his peevish shout: 'Come back *here*, Foxy!'

This other voice beyond the trees held all the promise that his entreaties lacked. It wafted on her ears once more, then receded. Here now on this heavenly common, scented with fox, rabbit, badger and squirrel, was the brightest sward of grass she had ever seen. She wrenched off a few blades and chewed. Ah, the piquancy of succulent, wholesome grass! It was the emetic she needed; she wanted to be sick. Agonizingly, she retched. A sharp ache sprang back and forth from her throat to her ribs, but the vomit would not come. Here was a sprinkling of rabbit droppings. She rolled over on her back in the middle of the brown spheres, intent upon ridding herself of the vicarage odour, upon giving herself a wild scent to suit her newfound liberty. The vicar's loosened, yet still clinging, woollen coat exasperated her. Then stronger rabbit smells led her through a briar clump, which tore that coat from her back. Now she really felt free. Finding more rabbit stools she rolled again, squirming her spine luxuriously If only she could be rid of her collar, too. It was too tight.

'Fox-y! Fox-y!' The vicar's voice, echoing from the hill path above her, seemed to be coming from another world, a world to which she could not, must not return.

Try-hy-hy-hy! came the haunting voice from the opposite direction. On she ran — away from the vicar's summons, towards the song beyond. Once again she wore the demeanour of the young huntress. But, oh, how unfit! How she panted! Yet, in her present rapture, she quite forgot the discomfort of her vicarage corpulence.

* * *

The Reverend Richard Illingworth entered his sitting-room still breathing heavily from the effort of his unaccustomed walk and in spite of the brief respite of the car journey. 'Good morning!' he said, rather sheepishly.

'Hallo I'm Rose Peterson.'

Illingworth's crimson features shifted into a blend of smile and grimace. 'I know you are. You've come for Foxy! Well, I'm afraid Foxy is lost.'

'Lost?' exclaimed Rose, flabbergasted. Not again! she was thinking. Oh, no, not again? She got up and faced the man. 'Where? Where is she lost?'

'On Raynham Common. She tugged so hard, I let her off the lead. And well — she just ran off. I shouted till I was hoarse, then I got worried about keeping you waiting.'

The vicar's manner annoyed Rose. 'You asked me to be here at nine,' she said coldly, 'now it's nearly ten.'

The Reverend Richard pulled back his cuff, glanced at his watch and pursed his lips. 'I'm sure there's no urgency, Mrs Peterson . . .'

Rose stifled her anger and sighed. This man had lost her

dog, yet informed her there was no urgency. 'I'd like to be shown the place where you last saw my terrier — straight away, please. There's no need for you to stay after that. I'll do the searching.'

Seeing how adamant she was the vicar conceded defeat. 'Oh, all right then,' he said sulkily. 'It's only a few minutes in the car and less than five minutes walk on the common. But I must warn you, Mrs Peterson, it's very inhospitable there, very inhospitable.'

Rose was already at the front door, impatiently tapping her knuckles with her car keys with an anger she could only just control.

Oh, what a tiresome, unyielding sort of girl, thought Illingworth, worse than Monica!

* * *

Freed of lead and lap-dog coat, stinking of her old rabbit character, leaping over the wild ground, Gannet felt an ecstatic sense of liberation, like a songbird freed from a trap. The wind had stilled almost completely, and all other sounds became distinct. Another two hundred yards and the enchanting voice impinged on her brain with total clarity. *Try-hy-hy-hy! Eleu, push 'im up!* it said. Then *Leu-leu-leu-leu! Huic to Jupiter then!* The syllables were followed by the dulcet music of a wind instrument — a hunting horn. Gannet was so happy at hearing the sound that she answered it by a series of barks, given with all the joy of an angel singing hallelujahs. Despite her somewhat unfit state, she scuttled faster than ever, pushing through the pale brown brambles, bouncing over the green-gold bracken, springing athwart the tussocks and the heather, always directly towards the huntsman's merry voice and horn.

A chorus followed the horn-notes, the silver-tongued high-fidelity of many dogs carefully bred to a uniform stamp, hound music like a peal of bells, an exuberant pack of twenty couples, breaking covert — on the trail of a fox cub. Gannet's white legs switched back and forth, rhythmic as clockwork, deliriously happy. *Forra-forra-forra-forrard!* the human voice urged the pack. Urged Gannet, too. She could see the leaders now, just like those lovely great hounds who had been her friends at Owlhurst, many, many months ago, so strong and gigantic, so lithe and majestic. They swung left-handed in front of her, a passionate avalanche of tan-and-white-and-black in the winter forest, all their senses concentrated on the just discernible trail from the fox's glands. As the huntsman's horn doubled for the third time, calling the tail-hounds out of covert, Gannet joined the main body of the pack, her soprano mingling with their contralto. But already her heart was pounding. Her jaws were wide open, desperately panting from her week and a half of idleness. But it didn't matter; she was involved in the most exciting, the most important thing in the world; she was in seventh heaven.

* * *

'It was here, just here, that I took her lead off,' the Reverend Richard was telling Rose. 'The naughty little thing simply bounded down the slope, not taking the slightest notice of me.'

'All right, Mr Illingworth. I'll find her.'

While the portly vicar took his leave and returned to his car, Rose started walking down the hillside, calling 'Gan-net! Gan-net!'

Then, hearing the huntsman's horn, she remembered that the Westdown's adjacent hunt, the Moakley Union, met in this direction close to Guildford on Saturdays. They would have been cubhunting since soon after dawn. Maybe her old Moakley Union friends, Dick and Marjorie Howard would be out? Of course, Gannet would be thrilled if she came across the hunt. Likely as not she'd join in the sport. Yes, that could easily be what had happened . . . She'd joined the hunt!

'Gan-net! Gan-net!'

Blast that silly vicar! Why couldn't he just have met her at nine, as arranged, instead of trying to be clever? Eight months of hit-and-miss and now this ridiculous situation, this irresponsibility! If only Luke was here to help her. Problems simply evaporated like mist before the sun when Luke was around. Rose resolved that, unless Gannet turned up very soon, she'd find a call-box and ring Luke and persuade him to drive over. His surgery was in the Moakley Union country. It wouldn't take him fifteen minutes.

Now she could hear the distant cry of hounds. She walked on a brisk pace, and where the heath turned into farmland she spotted them three hundred yards away, careering over the plough in their tight huddle. And there was a terrier struggling to keep up with them. Was it Gannet? It must be, it had to be . . . Yes, it *was* Gannet! But Rose was far behind.

* * *

When the hounds had run their fox for half a mile, a stretch of scent-obliterating sheep foil interrupted their career and Gannet, taking advantage of the check, lay on the grass behind them, panting feverishly, her whole body shuddering with exhaustion.

Two scarlet-coated equestrian figures, their horses' necks white with galloping lather, rode up, but kept a discreet distance from the hounds questing passionately this way and that for their quarry's line.

'Do you see that, Jack?' the huntsman called softly to his whipper-in. 'Got a terrier with 'em. Not a Moakley terrier, is it?'

'Looks familiar,' said the whipper-in, stroking his gelding's lathered neck.

'Not one as I'd recognise.'

'Similar to one I sees at the Westdown kennels year or two back.'

'Go on with yer, lad, you couldn't remember that.' All the time the two of them were watching the pack casting — with only half a mind on Gannet.

'Don't forget, I'm a terrier man. I can recall a terrier as quick and good as I remember a human face . . . Looks like one old Ted Jennings bred at Owlhurst, the Jack Russell their Rose had, their kennel-girl as married that nice vet fellow, Peterson. I heard she'd lost it.'

'It's a long shot, boy. There's dozens of terriers come and gone since then.'

'I'm telling you, I can pick 'em out like a copper remembers a thief. I remember it lost a couple of toes in a keeper's trap. That Rose brought it to our puppy and terrier show and all . . .'

As he spoke the Moakley hounds were on the scent again. 'There now, that's the line, Craftsman's got it. *Huic to Craftsman then!* Get on Jack, get yourself up to the Guildford road in double-quick time and see 'em safely over, right?'

'OK then,' said the whipper-in, spurring his perspiring horse into a canter again. 'But I swear it's that terrier,' he flung over his shoulder.

The mounted followers, having just jumped the posts-and-rails leading into the field behind were now closing up, a bevy of bobbing bowlers and velvet caps and hunting tweed, brown and bay horses, blacks and chestnuts, each rider determined to be first behind hounds, kicking up the turf as they landed.

This was proving an artful cub, running on a catchy scent. It seemed that every time hounds gained on him, he changed direction or crossed a wall, or ran through manure or brought them, for some reason or other, to another check. And at each momentary halt, Gannet grew a little weaker, a little more breathless. Now their quarry,. too, was growing weary of the chase. He was circling back towards his native covert on the common. Having crossed the Guildford road he described an arc over two fields of winter corn and three meadows, recrossing the same road five hundred yards up towards the town.

The followers were not used to this kind of sport on cubbing days. They thundered on to the road from the soggy turf, their horses' hooves changing of a sudden from squelch to clatter as they met the tarmac. The Master, seeing the fox crossing the highway less than two hundred yards in front, with the baying pack close on his brush, pulled his horse into a walk and held up his hand with two crisp commands: 'Hold hard! Be quiet, please!' The people he addressed were half hidden by the pull of their horses' steam. When all the hounds were safely over, the Master turned his horse's head towards a nearby five-bar gate, which would take his followers off the road and up with the hounds again; deftly lifting the latch with the bone handle of his whip, he led the way through.

The last rider in the column was a man, whose blood mare had nearly brought him down at the posts-and-rails before the first check. He had been barred from riding with the Westdown hunt following an incident at a Boxing Day meet, and already suffered from a somewhat murky reputation with the Moakley. His name was Leonard Trench.

Just ahead was another thorn hedge barrier with, inset, a hunt jump known as a tiger trap, a low combination of timber rails. On the far side hounds careered straight across the front of that obstacle. The field Master held up his hand, waited for the pack to pass, then goaded his horse at the jump. The others followed his bold and confident lead. Only one rider was left behind. Taking up the rear, Trench presented his mare at the obstacle so ineptly that she refused. Beating her across the quarters he went at it again. She jumped. But a sudden flash of tan-and-white on the landing side frightened the horse, causing her to peck at the top rails like a mad thing. Trench saw that flash of tan-and-white, too. But he didn't know it was Gannet.

The mare pitched Trench on to the plough and, as he fell, she rolled heavily across his back, then got to her feet and galloped after the others, stirrup-irons flapping crazily against her flanks. Trench lay where he had fallen, quite motionless. Two foot-followers who witnessed the incident ran up and took a look at him. One of them then walked at a very fast pace to the nearest telephone-box to summon an ambulance.

The hounds were well ahead now, out of Gannet's sight, but she could still hear their distant, excited cry, which lured her on inexorably, on through wire and hedge and scrub, on over ditch and stream, on across pasture and plough. Like the hounds' mouths her mouth was wide open, but whereas their jaws were spread in song, hers were expanded in hectic breathing. Propelled like a wound-up machine, aching in every limb, yet with a passion for the chase that overrode the physical signals that warned her to stop, Gannet's little legs flicked back and forth as though her life depended, not — as it surely did — on resting, but on galloping to take part in the finish.

At last the fox closed on a beloved refuge high up on the common and, minutes later, Gannet knew from the change in the hounds' vocal expression that they were marking to ground. Old instinct telling her, too, that when foxhounds reach their quarry's lair it is the terrier's turn for glory, she put the last ounce of effort into her pace. In straining thus she felt a terrible pain sear through her heart. She was trotting with short paces now, head hung low, jaws open at right angles, tail clenched between her buttocks, agony written in her eyes.

It was a very large earth with half a dozen entrances, a sandy earth, perhaps begun by rabbits, enlarged by badgers and only recently occupied by foxes. Some of the hounds, enshrouded in clouds of sweaty vapour, raised their heads and howled for the blood they demanded as their right, some chose an entrance to claw and threaten, others reclined regaining their breath, anticipating the bolt. Gannet, notwithstanding her desperation, but rather recognizing this as her moment of triumph, squeezed past a hound that half blocked an entrance with its great muddy head.

But no sooner was she close to the earth's mouth then her

body was seized with a paralysis, an insensibility, forcing her to lie on her flank, panting heavily.

'Hallo, hallo, you're a plucky little thing, aren't you, eh?' said the huntsman, riding up to the earth and seeing Gannet lying full length, rib-cage heaving, while the hounds crowded the clay over the point where their quarry lay.

'I told you so!' The whipper-in came up minutes later, throwing himself quickly from the saddle. 'It's that Westdown terrier all right. I can see where the claws are missing, plain as the nose on my face. Here, little bitch, let's see what your collar tells us.'

Gannet raised her head towards the voice. But these were strangers, and her stark experiences, telling her to value and safeguard her new-found freedom, rang alarm through her diminutive frame. Thanks to this brief rest at the earth she had recovered some of her strength. On her feet in a trice, she vanished into the depths of the woody heathland at an aching trot.

Although she had been happy enough at Ripley Manor with her spaniel companions and nursing her litter of puppies, and although the Reverend Richard and his daily cleaner had imprisoned her successfully, thwarting her attempt to escape, the determination to go home, home to Rose and the security of her birthplace, had never really deserted her. The refrain that now kept singing in her head was: *'East, east! Go east!'*

So predominant in her senses was her aim to push eastwards that it helped to quell the awful ache that now gripped her entire body.

The huntsman was on the point of lifting his hounds — tired, muddy and deprived of their fugitive — away from the earth and home to kennels when Rose strode up the slope saying: 'You didn't see a terrier here, did you, a smooth-haired Jack Russell?'

Touching his cap politely the whipper-in answered. 'Mrs Peterson? We did and all. Your bitch Gannet it was. Recognized her from the missing claws.'

'You've got one hell of a memory,' said Rose.

'She's a beauty I'd never forget. But I reckon she's at the end of her tether now.'

'Where is she?'

The whipper-in pointed down the birch-dotted slope of the common. 'She scampered off that way.'

Rose started in the same direction. She trailed round the heath and the woods, calling until her voice, echoing faintly back at her, cracked. Then she retrieved her car, drove to the vicarage and, with a distinctly sardonic tone, asked Illingworth if he'd be so kind as to inform her straight away if Gannet turned up there.

Walking back towards her car she had another thought. Even after all these months Gannet's instinct just might guide her towards Owlhurst, in the direction of the place of her puppyhood. She remembered some time ago Luke saying that was a strong probability. In which case Gannet would be moving in a bee-line — as straight as the terrain would allow — that way now. Rose went to her car and consulted the map. Owlhurst wasn't more than ten miles across country and she was in a mood to make any sacrifice to retrieve Gannet alive. Her dog could run into all sorts of hazards on the way and she would never forgive herself if Gannet suffered some awful accident at this stage.

She returned to Illingworth, asked to borrow his telephone, contacted Ted Jennings, and informed him she intended to hike from Raynham Common to Owlhurst and that, allowing for stops and searching she'd be in by four. She rang Luke and told him the same thing, overruling all his objections softly but firmly one by one.

She drove to the point on the common road nearest to the fox's earth where Gannet was last seen, put on her wellingtons, tucked the map into her anorak and started walking. Every few hundred yards she stopped and searched, looking briefly up that path or down that stream valley. After about a mile it began to rain and after a mile and a half it was raining so hard she took shelter in a barn and cursed her luck. She could think of nothing but Gannet. All the old visions of her beloved terrier came back to her, visions and memories that had been largely erased from her mind through her preoccupation with courtship, wedding and honeymoon, and with thoughts of making a home and of her new life.

Now she focused on the mystery of how Gannet had got from that canal to London and from London to Somerset and what adventures she must have experienced in reaching Mrs Bowes-Onslow. And she marvelled again at what an extraordinary piece of good fortune it was that Mrs Bowes-Onslow had put her in for a terrier show and that Derek Fowles had recognized her and told Ted. Then she recalled this morning's hunt and how much it must have exhausted poor Gannet. She reckoned that if she was making her way to Owlhurst Gannet would be dead beat by now. Yet given the dismal rain, the more she considered the chance of her terrier making for her native kennels, the less likely it seemed to be.

When the rain grew lighter and the sun shone through she emerged from the barn and strode on, congratulating herself each time the villages and other major landmarks tallied with the map. She was less than two miles from Owlhurst, however, when disaster struck.

Coming to a locked gate she knew well, she climbed it and jumped confidently from the top. But, landing awkwardly on a cattle rut, she twisted the same ankle with which she had been admitted to hospital a year before, after falling into the gravel pit. She started hobbling very slowly across the next field, just touching the ground for balance with the toe of her bad foot. Twenty minutes later she found a strong stick which she used as a support, but it didn't help her get along any faster. Her face was white as a sheet from the torture of it.

She glanced at her watch and shook her head despondently. It was no good; she'd never reach the kennels by dark at this rate; she had to get to a telephone. Maybe if she rested it for a while, she thought, it would improve. She sat on a bank, foot raised, and nursed the offending ankle, which seemed to her to have swollen to twice the size. She closed her eyes, lay back on the bank and tried to relax. When she opened them again, she could not at first believe what she witnessed.

Peering down the line of the bank she saw, about two hundred yards off, a tan-and-white terrier. It seemed — in the gloaming and through the mist of her eyes brought on by the pain — to be a mirage. It was walking towards her, not alert and bright as a terrier would normally be in rabbit-filled farmland such as this, but drop-eared, tired, slow-paced, panting. Rose shook her head and blinked. Yes, it was a terrier, but it couldn't be Gannet because Gannet would be going the other way — towards Owlhurst.

But then — some way behind the terrier — came the figures of two men. There was no mistaking them. Luke and Ted. Then Rose knew. Gannet had reached Owlhurst and was leading the search party for her, just as she had led the way to the gravel pit a year before. All Rose's anxiety dropped away as though it had never been; she didn't even notice the agony of her ankle. *'Ganny, Ganny, Gan-net!'*

At the sound of Rose's voice Gannet's whole body and demeanour suddenly transformed, brightened as though from the infusion of some joyous electricity, and with a little yelp and a wriggle she dashed forward, ears pricked. She hesitated for a moment, as though the sound may have been a trick. But, within what seemed like only a split second after that, Rose felt her terrier's paws pummelling her chest and the eager ecstasy of her little pink tongue all across her face, and she heard nothing, not even her husband's voice, but the little dog's squeals of unbridled joy.

While the gentle beauty of Rose's voice became more real to Gannet with every passing moment, so the girl's touch and smell and loving aura grew stronger too. And, as she passionately licked the tears from Rose's cheeks, she knew her travels were over forever.